Finding the Right Words

*A Weekly Portion
of Shemiras HaLashon*

Finding the Right Words

A Weekly Portion
of Shemiras HaLashon

Rosally Saltsman

TARGUM/FELDHEIM

Published by:
Targum Press, Inc.
22700 W. Eleven Mile Rd.
Southfield, MI 48034
E-mail: targum@netvision.net.il
Fax toll free: 888-298-9992
www.targum.com

Distributed by:
Feldheim Publishers
202 Airport Executive Park
Nanuet, NY 10954

Printed in Israel

Rabbi Zev Leff

Rabbi of Moshav Matisyahu

Rosh Hayeshiva Yeshiva Gedola Matisyahu

הרב זאב לף

מרא דאתרא מושב מתתיהו

ראש הישיבה ישיבה גדולה מתתיהו

I have read the manuscript of the book *Finding the Right Words* by Rosally Saltsman, and I have found it inspiring and enjoyable.

Each generation has specific mitzvos that it embraces with extra enthusiasm. The mitzvah of *shemiras halashon* given impetus by the writings and teachings of Rav Yisroel Meir HaCohen Kagan — the Chafetz Chaim *zt"l*, has been observed with renewed fervor in our generation. *Shemiras halashon* study groups have been established in almost every Jewish community, yearly rallies are held in Eretz Yisrael and in the diaspora, and many *sefarim* have been published in various languages on the halachos, *hashkafos*, and *mussar* of guarding one's tongue properly.

Rosally Saltsman gleans from each *sidrah* observations and lessons pertinent to *shemiras halashon* that are interesting, informative, inspiring, and motivating. Everyone is entitled to present their individual Torah understandings and insights as long as they do not contradict true Torah, halachah, and *hashkafah*. I have found the *divrei Torah* contained in this book to fit these criteria, and I recommend this book as an enhancement to the great mitzvah of *shemiras halashon*.

May *Hashem Yisbarach* bless the author spiritually, physically, and materially as is due one who bestows merit on the masses of *Klal Yisrael*.

החותם לכבוד מזכי הרבים

Sincerely,

Rav Zev Leff

May this book be an *ilui neshamah* for:

My parents,
Maurice and Anna Saltsman
משה לייזר בן ברוך
חנה בת קלמן
Moshe Lazar ben Baruch
Chana bas Kalman

My uncle, **Israel Leitman**
ישראל בן קלמן
Yisrael ben Kalman

Sydney Klaiman
שמעון בן שמואל
Shimon ben Shmuel

Stephen Klaiman
שמואל בן שמעון
Shmuel ben Shimon

Norman Cuttler
שמואל נטע הלוי בן לייב
Shmuel Notte HaLevi ben Leib

And may this book serve as a *zechus* for *Am Yisrael*
and help bring Hashem's mercy upon us and speed
the coming of Mashiach *bimheirah beyameinu,*
Amen.

Contents

Devarim

Foreword

by Rabbi Paysach J. Krohn

Dear Reader,

You are about to embark on a trip through the *parashios* of the Torah riding a very special train. You will venture from week to week and find at every station wondrous lessons about *shemiras halashon*. The association to the particular parashah is at times clever, at times creative, and at times obvious. In any case you will find Rosally Saltsman's thoughts informative, instructional, and well researched.

Ms. Saltsman is an exceptional writer whose articles have appeared in various publications. This book was written with both adult and youngster in mind. Thus, it can be read at a Shabbos table, or even as a nighttime lesson before a child goes to sleep.

Rav Simcha Wasserman, *zt"l*, once told me that there is a specific reason Hashem has chosen to make *shemiras halashon* the "mitzvah of our generation." *Chazal* tell us (*Yoma* 9a) that the second Beis HaMikdash was destroyed because of *sinas chinam* (baseless and senseless hatred). Thus unless we uproot that sin from *Klal Yisrael*, Hashem finds it difficult to bring Mashiach. We must foster *ahavas chinam* (love of a fellow Jew for no other reason than he or she is Jewish) to enable Mashiach to come, and a major step in that direction is when people abide by the laws of *shemiras halashon*.

The Chafetz Chaim writes that it is a mistake to think that *shemiras halashon* deals only with spreading slander. In his *sefer Chovas HaShemirah* he enumerates ten things that comprise violations of *shemiras halashon*. Among them are anger, haughtiness, lying, mocking, and using words that pain others in conversation. This book finds references to these flaws in the *parashios* and suggests guidance in how to avoid them.

There is a plethora of material available today about *shemiras halashon*. Books, tapes, videos, stickers, magnets, etc. — each play a role in our need to be constantly reminded of the magnitude of *shemiras halashon*. May this book bring all of us one step closer, week by week, to *ahavas Yisrael* and the witnessing of Mashiach in our time.

Respectfully,
Paysach J. Krohn

Acknowledgments

There are always many people to thank in any creative endeavor, and I, as many others before me and many others after me, cannot hope to express my gratitude properly to everyone who has had some input into the writing of this book.

I would like to thank Hashem *Yisbarach* for giving me the opportunity to write this book and orchestrating events so as to make it possible for me to do so. I would like to thank Rabbi Zelig Pliskin, whose book *Guard Your Tongue* started me on the path to a whole new way of speaking. My deep gratitude to Rabbi Zev Leff, who dedicated the time to read this manuscript and its revisions and agreed to give his *haskamah*. Words cannot properly express my appreciation to Rabbi Paysach Krohn, who gave generously of his time, insights, and encouragement. They have all been invaluable and inspiring. I am truly grateful.

Thank you to my wonderful friends who have lovingly supported both my spiritual and creative endeavors, which I hope come together in this manuscript. To my teacher, Rochel Bryna Frumin, who has been a lighthouse on my spiritual path, I offer sincere thanks. Thanks to Veeda (Chaya) Margol, who has been a roadmap on my path, and Esti Allina Turnauer, who has been the navigator. A very special thanks to Hanoch Levin.

My appreciation goes to Ronni Kives, who burned the midnight oil to proofread and edit. To Ruty Malovany, who has been my spiritual mentor, and Bea Rozenblum, who has encouraged me to add another book to her *gemach*. And of course my gratitude goes to the good people at Targum.

To my son, Joshua (Yehoshua Yisrael), who is both my greatest teacher and my greatest student, I thank you for the joy you have constantly brought to my life and I dedicate this book to you. May your words and deeds always be positive and always be a source of blessing in this world and the next, as they have been to my life. May you live your life in a way that personifies *kiddush shem Shamayim* in good physical and spiritual health till 120!

לשוני עט סופר מהיר :

My tongue is like a
pen of a skillful scribe.

Tehillim 45:2

Introduction

When someone speaks *lashon hara* he commits up to thirty-one sins with each utterance. Similarly when someone abstains from speaking *lashon hara*, especially when the opportunity to do so presents itself, he fulfills up to thirty-one mitzvos — including "*lo tirtzach*" (Thou shalt not commit murder), since slandering someone can ultimately lead to their untimely death. Also, one Jew who causes another to lose his livelihood is considered to have murdered him (*Yevamos* 78b). And embarrassing someone, also a result of *lashon hara*, is considered akin to murder. Whoever publicly embarrasses his fellowman is considered as if he has shed blood, because shame causes a person's blood to drain from his face (*Bava Metzia* 58b).

The Vilna Gaon wrote that whoever refrains from speaking *lashon hara* merits the hidden light of the next world, which even the angels cannot see.

Lashon hara (and its sub-categories: *rechilus, motzi shem ra,* etc.) constitutes any speech, true or false, which is negative about or can have negative implications for others, individually or as a group, whether or not it includes oneself. *Lashon hara* can harm a fellow Jew whether or not this was the intention. The harm could be financial, physical, emotional, psychological, or social. The repercussions affect the speaker, the listener, and the person being discussed, and multiply exponentially with each retelling.

Lashon hara should not be spoken about anyone, regardless of familial proximity. Although the halachah relates to Jews, it is considered meritorious to speak positively about everyone (unless they are known as evil).

Even objects are considered to possess a spiritual essence, according to Kabbalistic literature. Our negative thoughts and words even about inanimate objects, animals, and plants have been shown to influence them negatively, and each negative thought we think and word we utter has a negative affect on our souls and on our chances for success in our endeavors, as *Chazal* have so often cited. It is not the purpose of this book to delve into negative mindsets. However, whoever practices the highly esteemed character trait and sadly neglected mitzvah of *shemiras halashon* will discover a greater sense of well-being and greater positivity enhancing his life. The obligation of guarding one's speech applies to men, women, and children alike, regardless of age or position.

In Rav Zelig Pliskin's book *Happiness*, he gives an interesting exercise. Think of an imaginary person and for three minutes only say good things about him (to yourself). Now imagine a person and for three minutes say only bad things about him (to yourself). Feel the difference? When you speak positively about someone, you yourself feel good, and when you speak negatively about someone, you yourself feel bad. When we speak *lashon hara*, we are also harming ourselves.

The sin of *lashon hara* is so great that it is alluded to in each of the *parashios* (the weekly readings) of the Torah. It is the intention of this book, *b'ezras Hashem*, to discuss the occurrence of the laws regarding *shemiras halashon* as they appear in each parashah of the Torah.

For reasons of simplicity I will be using the pronouns

"he" and "his" throughout the book. Most of the references and quotations have been taken from the Stone edition of the Artscroll Chumash, published by Mesorah Publications.

This book is not meant to be a halachic treatise. Any questions regarding individual incidents of *lashon hara* should be directed to a competent halachic authority.

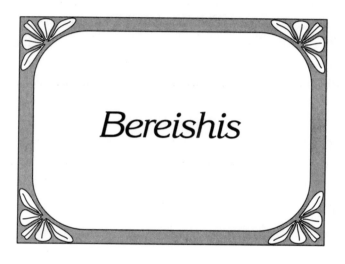

Bereishis

"איזהו גיבור? הכובש את יצרו."

One of the *perushim* of the first *pasuk* of *Bereishis* —
בראשית ברא אלוקים את... — is that God created the alphabet,
"את," referring to the letters *alef* through *taf*. First God created the alphabet and language, and then He created the
sky and the land with ten utterances. Therefore the above
saying from *Chazal* gets an additional meaning. Who is
strong? He who conquers his *yetzer* to misuse his words, his
"את."

Parashas

Bereishis

"In the beginning..." (*Bereishis* 1:1) there was no *lashon hara*.

Have you ever noticed that all of life's problems resulted from the first sin of *lashon hara*? The snake spoke *lashon hara* against God. Chavah spoke *lashon hara* against the snake. Adam spoke *lashon hara* against Chavah. Notice how even the first case of *lashon hara* snowballed? Had there been more people it would probably have continued, but as things were, there was no one left to blame. Since then, we must work hard for a living, endure pain in childbirth, raise children with difficulties, and have marital discord, all because of the sin of *lashon hara*.

The punishment for eating from the tree of knowledge was death. Adam and Chavah increased their sins (and punishment) by not taking responsibility for their actions. Instead they blamed each another. This problem is prevalent today as well. A large portion of *lashon hara* is caused by the unwillingness of people to take responsibility for their own actions. Taking responsibility, and not blaming others, is one of the prerequisites for living in the Garden of Eden.

Parashas

Noach

Before bringing a flood upon the earth, God gave the generation of the flood a chance to repent. But they didn't. On the contrary, they laughed at Noach building the ark. It stands to reason that they also spoke *lashon hara* about him. Imagine the conversations in the pubs, the scorn and ridicule every time it rained.

Then the flood came and they stopped laughing. They stopped talking *lashon hara*, and they ultimately stopped talking. After a year, Noach and his family — what was left of humanity — left the ark. And what happened? Cham spoke *lashon hara* about his father. The sin in and of itself was terrible, of course, but what was worse was that Cham hadn't learned the lesson of the generation of the flood. They laughed at Noach and he laughed at Noach. They spoke against Noach and he spoke against Noach.

So an obvious question presents itself: How can it be that the son of the most righteous man of his time, who was well aware of the consequences of *lashon hara*, both from Adam himself and from witnessing the end of the generation of the flood, would not internalize the lesson and abstain from speaking *lashon hara*?

Perhaps it's because he thought that if it's within the family it's not *lashon hara*. After all, whom did he tell? His brothers. Wives tell secrets to husbands. Children tell parents. It doesn't count, we think. But it does. Our ability to harm is greater when we speak to and about the people who are closest to us. What we say is more readily believed and people are hurt more quickly and deeply by those close to them than by strangers. *Lashon hara* within Noach's family destroyed it from the inside, something a year dwelling among animals wasn't able to do. Cham made a big mistake. Let us learn to internalize the lesson.

Parashas

Lech Lecha

We learn from *parashas Lech Lecha* how important it is to be specific in order to avoid misunderstandings. At the beginning of the parashah, God commands Avraham to go, to leave his country, his birthplace, and his father's house, to a country which God Himself will show him. Why the need for all the detail? To teach us that every word we say is important and when we say something, the more specific we are, the less chance there is of misunderstandings occurring. When it comes to which land Hashem wants Avraham to go to, Hashem goes as far as to show Avraham Himself.

How many arguments include the words "But I thought you meant..."? How much *lashon hara* is caused by ambiguity or by one word misquoted and substituted for another? And just in case we didn't get the message at the beginning of the parashah, Hashem teaches it again at the end of the parashah. He changes Avram's name to "Avraham" and Sarai's name to "Sarah." Not only a word, but even a letter makes a difference. We know this from all the interpretations of the Torah through the use of *gematria*.

Many tragedies have been brought upon the Jewish people through a misplaced word; the story of Kamtza and Bar Kamtza is one very significant instance of misunderstanding that led to national tragedy. Some religions go as far as to "prove" that the Jews should be destroyed by misquoting the Bible. We need to choose our words — every word — carefully, and in so doing, we emulate God.

Parashas
Vayeira

The classic example of avoiding *lashon hara* (quoted by Rashi) is God's misquoting Sarah when He tells Avraham that she laughed, saying she has grown too old to have a child. In fact she had said that Avraham (her husband) has grown too old to have a child.

> And Sarah laughed at herself, saying, "After I have withered shall I again have delicate skin? And my husband is old!"
>
> Then Hashem said to Avraham, "Why is it that Sarah laughed saying: 'Shall I in truth bear a child though I have aged?' "
>
> *(Bereishis 18:12–13)*

God does this to keep *shalom bayis* between Avraham and Sarah. If God can misquote someone for the sake of keeping peace, surely we are expected to go to great lengths to avoid saying anything that would cause conflict between any two people, particularly between a husband and wife.

There is another example of *shemiras halashon* in the parashah. While we are required to warn someone of imminent danger, halachah says that if there is a way to do so without speaking *lashon hara*, we are not permitted to speak *lashon hara* but must choose the alternative way of protecting him.

Parashas Vayeira is full of people who are miraculously saved from certain death at the last minute by virtue of God's *chesed*. *Chazal* say that life and death are in the hands of the tongue, i.e., what one says and what one doesn't say.

When the two angels come to Sedom, Lot is at the gate waiting for them. He greets them much as Avraham did, pleading with them to return with him to his home, where he will show them hospitality so they won't have to be out on the street. What he doesn't say is that were they to stay on the street, their lives would be in danger.

Once they are inside his house, he is willing to endanger his family to protect them. Wouldn't it have been easier to just warn them of the danger in Sedom and send them on their way? Wouldn't he be justified to have told of the terrible things Sedomites did to those who entered their gates? Possibly, but Lot felt he had a choice. He decided to protect the "visitors" himself and thereby avert the need to speak *lashon hara* about the people of Sedom.

At first the "guests" refused to go with Lot and said, "No, rather we will spend the night in the square."

> And he urged them very much, so they turned toward him and came to his house.
>
> *(Bereishis 19:3)*

Lot didn't say to himself, "Well, this isn't working. I'd better tell them the truth." Instead, he urged them until they relented and came to his home.

And what's the next thing that happens? Lot is saved and becomes the scion of two nations, through one of which King David and Mashiach will come.

Sometimes it's not what you say, but what you don't say that can make the difference between life, death, and eternity.

Chayei Sarah

After many years of marriage, Avraham comes to do the last *chesed* with his wife. He wants to bury her in Me'aras HaMachpeilah. In spite of the great sadness that he felt at Sarah's passing, Avraham was very careful regarding the deal he made with Efron. He insists that Efron accept payment from him even though Efron is willing to give the land to Avraham as a gift.

> And Efron replied to Avraham, saying to him: "My lord, heed me! Land worth four hundred silver shekels, between me and you — what is it? Bury your dead."
>
> Avraham heeded Efron, and Avraham weighed out to Efron the price which he had mentioned in the hearing of the children of Cheis.
>
> *(Bereishis 23:14–16)*

There are three points which are connected to *lashon hara* in this section.

1) The conversation between Efron and Avraham was conducted "in the hearing of the children of Cheis." This is mentioned a number of times. It is clear that Avraham was very careful regarding what he said and did because he knew that every word was being heard and he wanted to avoid a misunderstanding.

"Hillel said... Do not make a statement that cannot be easily understood on the grounds that it will be understood eventually" (*Pirkei Avos* 2:5). When Efron speaks he says, "*L'einei b'nei ami* — In the view of the children of my people," while Avraham says, "*B'aznei am ha'aretz* — In the hearing of the members of the council."

2) "Avraham heeded Efron." But Efron told Avraham that he was giving him the land as a gift, so how did Avraham heed him? The intent is that Avraham really did heed him because he "heard" what Efron wanted, that he pay him four hundred shekel. Why would Efron mention the sum of the land if it were a gift? People don't generally tell you how much a gift is worth. Also, Efron puts himself first, saying, "between me and you." It was clear to Avraham

that he was thinking of his own interests first.

3) The Or HaChaim says that Avraham didn't want anyone years later or generations later to say that Me'aras HaMachpeilah didn't rightfully belong to him. So in order to prevent any future disparaging remarks, he paid for the land and also received it as a gift just to make sure so that no one would come later with the claim that the land isn't his. Avraham saw the future. "Go out and discern which is the proper way to which a man should cling... Rabbi Shimon says: One who considers the outcome of a deed" (*Pirkei Avos* 2:13).

Toward the end of the parashah it is written, "The field that Avraham had bought from the children of Cheis, there Avraham was buried and Sarah, his wife." Why is it mentioned again that Avraham paid for the cave, and why is it not written that Avraham and Sarah were buried in the cave that Avraham bought? Why is the purchase mentioned first? To emphasize that first Avraham bought the property and only when it was his did he bury his wife and was later buried there.

We can learn a lot about *lashon hara* from Avraham's behavior. Even when we're upset or grieving or in any other extreme emotional state, we have to be careful of what we say, be aware of who is listening to our words, hear not only what is said but what's implied, and make sure that our deeds don't leave an opening for someone to speak *lashon hara* about us even in the distant future. We must ensure that we are understood, we must demonstrate understanding, and we must see the results of our deeds.

The rewards for guarding one's speech include longevity. We should all merit the long life of Sarah Imeinu.

Parashas

Toldos

"**C**ursed be they who curse you, and blessed be they who bless you" (*Bereishis* 27:19) — this is part of the blessing that Yaakov Avinu receives from his father.

The Baal Shem Tov would say that other people serve as a mirror for us. Whenever we see a negative trait in someone else it is because we have it in ourselves. If someone sees the good in someone else it is because he himself is worthy. What Yizchak Avinu says is not only a blessing but a fact: Whoever sees something to curse in another person is in fact cursing himself, and whoever sees something to praise in another person is in fact blessing himself.

When someone speaks *lashon hara*, three people are called to trial in Heaven: the person speaking, the person listening, and the person being spoken about. Therefore if someone speaks *lashon hara* about someone else, thereby cursing him, he brings punishment upon himself. One who finds the good in others and defends them against *lashon hara* by giving them the benefit of the doubt and finding favor for them, protects himself from Divine judgment.

The way the blessing is phrased provides evidence for the opinion that Yizchak knew very well whom he was blessing. He knew that Yaakov would be the victim of Esav's enmity once the latter discovered that Yaakov had taken the blessings. Therefore Yitzchak blessed Yaakov in such a way that would protect him from Esav's retribution, and the Jewish people have been protected by that blessing ever since. Such is the power of words, be they a blessing or a curse.

> Esav thought, "May the days of mourning for my father draw near, then I will kill my brother Yaakov."
> When Rivka was told of the words of her eldest son Esav, she sent and summoned Yaakov her younger son.
> *(Bereishis 27:41–42)*

If Esav only thought about what he was going to do, how did Rivka hear about it? According to Rashi, Esav's intention was revealed to her by *ruach hakodesh*. Here God does the opposite of what he did with Sarah and Avraham. For the sake of *shalom bayis*, and to save Yaakov's life, God decides to reveal to Rivka Esav's evil intentions. This is not *lashon hara* because it's for a constructive purpose — *pikuach nefesh*.

But, here God doesn't speak to her directly as in the beginning of the parashah when she came to ask about the child she was carrying and was told that she had twins. Here He reveals the information to her through *ruach hakodesh*. There is a halachah that if we have to reveal information to someone for a constructive purpose, if there is a way to do so other than telling them directly, we should employ that method instead. This is just what God Himself does.

Parashas

Vayeitzei

I t is difficult for us to understand how Rachel was willing to let Leah take her place and wed Yaakov. Imagine her pain watching her sister marry the man she loved and was hoping to build a home with. She sacrificed so much, everything that mattered to her, in order not to humiliate her sister under the *chupah*. Rachel gave Leah the signs that she and Yaakov had arranged between them, to save her sister that humiliation. She was also saving her father humiliation, because surely Yaakov would have refused to go through with the wedding as soon as he realized that he had been misled.

Rachel understood her sister's pain. She almost certainly heard her sister crying and praying not to be wed to Esav. And Rachel knew, even as she let him marry her sister, that Yaakov loved her and not Leah.

It's reasonable to assume that it was easier for Rachel to

empathize with Leah and show her such generosity of spirit exactly because she knew what she was going through. Perhaps if we were privy to what others were going through, it would be easier for us not to embarrass them by speaking *lashon hara* about them.

Until today, women go to Rachel's tomb to pour out their hearts and tears at the burial place of the compassionate matriarch because they believe that Rachel would understand their pain. She knew the anguish of giving up the man she loved, she knew the emptiness of childlessness, and she knew how to show compassion the way she did for her sister. Rachel Imeinu also holds out the hope that through compassion, one can still merit a husband and children.

Perhaps before we think of speaking negatively about someone, we could imagine the trials they are enduring. Perhaps they are suffering financial difficulties, marital problems, physical pain, or a loss of some kind. Perhaps like Leah they have some external sign of their suffering that we'd notice if we paid attention. Surely then we would find it easy not to cause them further anguish by speaking ill of them. May we all merit the compassion and understanding that exemplify Rachel Imeinu.

Parashas

Vayishlach

T here are two instances in the parashah where Yaakov Avinu tries to protect his family. In the first instance, he is returning home and is about to meet his brother Esav, whom he hasn't seen in twenty years and assumes is still angry with him. Therefore he divides his camp in order to protect his wives and children. He doesn't explain, warn, or talk about Esav; he acts.

In the second instance, after the incident with Shechem, an argument ensues between Yaakov and his sons. God enters into the argument and tells Yaakov to leave.

> God said to Yaakov, "Arise — go up to Beis-el and dwell there, and make an altar there to God Who appeared to you when you fled from Esav, your brother."
>
> *(Bereishis 35:1)*

God reminds Yaakov that when he fled from Esav and was trying to protect his family, the solution was to act. Here too, God implies that Yaakov shouldn't waste time arguing. He must leave this impure place and go to where God dwells. The answer is action, not talk.

There is no question but that we must protect ourselves from the evil intents of others, but this is better achieved through action than through talk, which can degenerate into *lashon hara*. (However, if it's necessary to speak in order to protect people, it may be permissible under certain circumstances.)

> And he (Esav) said, "Travel on and let us go — I will proceed alongside you."
>
> But he (Yaakov) said to him, "My lord knows that the children are tender, and the nursing flocks and cattle are upon me; if they will be driven hard for a single day, then all the flocks will die."
>
> *(Bereishis 33:12–13)*

According to the Talmud (*Moed Katan* 18a) Yaakov's primary concern was for his young children but delicacy did not permit him to speak of their possible death. As the

Sages put it, "a covenant is made with the lips," meaning that even an unintentional implication, an allusion, or a hint of something — all the more so an explicit statement — may become fulfilled as if it were prophecy. Such is the power of words.

This in fact happens when Rachel died as a result of Yaakov telling Lavan in the previous parashah: "With whomever you find your Gods, he shall not live" (*Bereishis* 31:32). Yaakov didn't know that Rachel had taken the statues and hidden them. Rachel died prematurely even though Lavan never found the statues with her. Rashi quotes the Sages as saying that even an unintentional curse uttered by the righteous is fulfilled. That's why people are careful to say "*b'ezras Hashem*" (God willing) or "*bli ayin hara*" (there should be no evil eye) when speaking of future events.

Vayeishev

Parashas *Vayeishev* is the beginning of a *lashon hara* marathon from many different sources. The parashah begins with Yosef speaking *lashon hara* against his brothers, which gets him into all kinds of trouble.

> And Yosef would bring evil reports about them to his father.

(Bereishis 37:2)

Immediately after, it's written: "Now Yisrael loved Yosef more than all his sons." It's hinted here that Yaakov didn't warn Yosef against speaking *lashon hara*, since he loved him more than all his sons and didn't find fault with him. Even though we love our children, we have to be careful in teaching them the laws of *shemiras halashon* and make sure they learn them and act accordingly. If we don't teach them properly they may quite literally, as well as figuratively, find themselves in a pit from which it would be difficult to extricate themselves. Yaakov suffered for twenty-two years because he didn't warn Yosef not to speak *lashon hara* about his brothers. Rashi is of the opinion that what Yosef said wasn't even true, that it was a misinterpretation of what he saw.

Another commentator, Abarbanel, says that "he brought evil reports" refers to evil reports which he heard about his brothers in the marketplace. These reports involved the sin of *rechilus* and perhaps even *motzi shem ra*. Although Yosef's being sold as a slave was part of a Divine plan to bring Yaakov's family to Egypt, the unfortunate circumstances through which this was carried out began with the sin of *lashon hara*.

The parashah begins:

> These are the chronicles of Yaakov: Yosef, at the age of seventeen, was a shepherd with his brothers by the flock, but he was a youth with the sons of Bilhah and the sons of Zilpah.
>
> *(Bereishis 37:2)*

Why does the parashah begin with the chronicles of Yaakov and then talk about Yosef? Because our *toldos*, the chronicles of our lives, are the legacy of our children. Our children's actions speak volumes about our lives. We have an obligation to ensure that their behavior reflects our priorities and values. That is the greatest way to show them our love.

In the episode where Yosef is sold, the brothers who tried to save him from death, Yehudah and Reuven, are named, whereas the brothers who conspired to kill him are not (*Oznaim LaTorah*). God purposely leaves this detail out, as its unnecessary inclusion would constitute *lashon hara*, bringing shame upon the tribes for eternity.

After the sale of Yosef, the brothers proclaimed a *cheirem*, a solemn ban forbidding anyone from divulging to Yaakov what had occurred (*Sefer Chassidim*, ed. *Mekitzei Nirdamim* #1562). This ban applied also to Yosef and to Yitzchak (who knew by prophetic vision what had happened). Rashi cites a midrash that even God was "bound" by the *cheirem*.

Both Potiphar's wife and Tamar wanted to be mothers of the children of Israel. According to the midrash,

Potiphar's wife had seen through astrology that she was destined to be an ancestor of Yosef's children. In the end it was her daughter, Osnat, who married Yosef.

However, the two women had very different ways of going about reaching their goals. Among the differences is that when Yehudah instructed that Tamar be burned for her "wanton" behavior, she didn't reveal that Yehudah was the father of her children (she was to have twins) but sent his property to him so that he could recognize it and identify it as his. The Sages taught (*Sotah* 10b) that she reasoned, "If he admits it voluntarily, well and good; if not, let them burn me, but let me not publicly disgrace him." According to Rashi, "One should let himself be thrown into a fiery furnace rather than expose his neighbor to public shame."

By the same token, Yehudah didn't use some excuse, which he could easily have found, to pardon Tamar without revealing the truth. He thought, "It is better for me to be shamed in this transient world than to be ashamed before my righteous fathers in the World to Come..." (*Targum Yonassan*). He therefore admitted to having fathered her children.

In stark contrast, Potiphar's wife (who is also not

named) feared that Yosef might report what had transpired, thereby disgracing her, and she preempted him, according to Ramban. Her *lashon hara* landed him in jail where he spent twelve years. God's original decree was for him to spend ten years in prison, one for each of the ten brothers he had slandered (*Seder Olam*; *Tanchuma*).

Parashas

Mikeitz

I t is difficult not to be amazed at the symmetry that exists between this parashah and the previous one. In the previous parashah, Yosef dreams a dream and interprets it: "Then they took him and cast him into the pit" (*Bereishis* 37:24). In this parashah, Pharaoh dreams a dream, Yosef interprets it, "and they rushed him from the pit" (41:14). In the previous parashah, Potiphar's wife tries to seduce Yosef. In this parashah, Yosef marries her daughter. In the previous parashah, Yosef pleads for his life with his brothers. In this parashah, they plead for their lives with him. In the previous parashah, Yosef goes down to Egypt, sold by his brothers as a slave. In this parashah, his brothers go down to Egypt and are ready to give themselves into slavery to Yosef. The symmetry is apparent in every verse as we see that what goes around comes around.

The brothers themselves are aware of poetic and Divine justice.

> They then said to one another, "Indeed we are guilty concerning our brother inasmuch as we saw his heart-felt anguish when he pleaded with us and we paid no heed; that is why this anguish has come upon us."
>
> *(Bereishis 42:21)*

Yet a few verses later it is written, "What is this that God has done to us?" (42:27). A few verses before, they admitted that they were guilty so why are they now asking what has God done to them?

Sometimes we are prepared to take responsibility for our actions but we are not willing to see how we have directly affected their results. If the brothers hadn't sold Yosef, Yosef could not have set his trap for them. This is a direct result of what the brothers did. We frequently fall into the traps that we set for ourselves. A word spoken at the wrong time, in the wrong place, snowballs until it blocks our path somewhere along the way. A pit that we dig for ourselves and then fall into is not a Divine punishment; rather, it is a punishment we have brought upon ourselves. God always makes sure that there is symmetry in the world — in nature and history, the wheel turns. We have to be very careful not to be ensnared by it.

In *Parashah Parables* (Bentsch Press), Rabbi Mordechai Kamenetzky quotes his grandfather, Rabbi Yaakov Kamenetsky, of blessed memory, who explained that Yosef had a very important message to send his brothers.

> More than a decade ago you sat in judgment. You thought you made a brilliant decision and were smarter than anyone else, including your father. You decided to sell me as a slave. Now you meet the saviour of the generation, the man who kept the world from starvation, and he is acting like a paranoid dictator. He is accusing you of something so bizarre that you think he has lost his mind. So is it not possible to think that you also made a gross error in judgment? Is it not possible that you saw the situation in a twisted light?

Do we not often do the very same thing? Do we not also judge people's speech and actions based on our limited understanding of a situation and then condemn them for it?

Vayigash

There are many conversations that are quoted in this parashah. A conversation between God and Yaakov, a conversation between Yosef and his brothers, between Yaakov's children and Yaakov, between Yaakov and Yosef, and between Yaakov and Pharaoh. There are so many recorded conversations about so many things that the conversation that is missing stands out: the explanation to Yaakov about what really happened to Yosef. When his sons tell Yaakov that Yosef is alive, it is written about Yaakov, "but his heart rejected it, for he could not believe them" (*Bereishis* 45:26). And honestly how could Yaakov believe them? Because if he believed them, he would have to believe that they had lied to him previously, and then he would have to ask them, "So what really happened to Yosef?"

After Yaakov Avinu got the good news, he goes to sacrifice before God. And God says to him: "Yosef shall place his hand on your eyes" (*Bereishis* 46:4). God doesn't give an explanation of how Yosef got to Egypt and Yaakov doesn't ask. Yaakov doesn't impose a condition, as he did when God spoke to him in an earlier parashah, and say, "If I receive an explanation of what happened to Yosef, I will go down to Egypt."

The meeting of Yosef and his father is one of the most poignant sections in *Tanach*.

> Then Yisrael said to Yosef, "Now I can die. After having seen your face, because you are still alive." And Yosef said to his brothers and to his father's household, "I will go up and tell Pharaoh, and I will say to him, 'My brothers and my father's household who were in the land of Canaan have come to me.' "
>
> (Bereishis 46:30–31)

What's going on here? A child doesn't see his father for twenty-two years, he hardly says a word to him and runs to tell Pharaoh that he's arrived? And puts him in Goshen far from the palace, in order to herd sheep? But it's written a few verses later that Yosef supported his father's entire household, so why did they have to herd sheep?

The meeting with Pharaoh is also strange. Pharaoh asks Yaakov how old he is and Yaakov blesses him. But we're waiting here for an explanation. What happened to Yosef? Why does Yaakov not ask someone, anyone? Why does no one tell him? The midrash relates that Yosef put Yaakov in Goshen so that he would have no opportunity to ask him what had transpired. That's devotion. He hadn't seen his father for twenty-two years and purposely stayed away from him, from the moment he arrived, in order not to upset him by speaking *lashon hara* about his brothers. What a *tikkun*!

Let's do some math. Yosef was seventeen years old when he was sold into slavery. Yaakov arrives in Egypt at age 130 and dies at 147 — that's seventeen years in Egypt. Yosef "brought evil reports" about his brothers to his father when he was seventeen years old and later, for seventeen years, avoided speaking evil about his brothers by not relating to Yaakov that he had been sold into slavery by them.

Nobody told Yaakov the truth — not God, not Pharaoh, not his children. Imagine for a moment how difficult it is to keep a secret known to so many people for so long. Especially for Yosef, who certainly didn't want his father to think that he had chosen not to see him for all this time.

It's likely that Yaakov figured out what had happened. After all, a very similar thing happened to him when he was forced to flee from his father and spend twenty years away from him. It's also possible that Yaakov was so grateful to see Yosef that he wanted to avoid the unpleasantness of thinking what might have passed between him and his brothers. Or he may have believed his children's story; after all, it is possible to escape from a wild animal and be thought dead. What's important is Yosef's devotion and commitment in keeping an incredibly difficult secret for seventeen years. Therefore, when it came Yaakov's time to die, he called Yosef, from among all his children, and had him swear to bury him among his ancestors. Yaakov understood that if Yosef could keep himself from speaking *lashon hara* for seventeen years, his oath could be depended upon. People who guard their tongues also keep their word.

There's another lesson in *shemiras halashon* that can be gleaned from Yaakov Avinu's meeting with Pharaoh.

Pharaoh said to Yaakov, "How many are the days of your life?" Yaakov answered Pharaoh, "The days of the years of my sojourns have been a hundred and thirty

years. Few and bad have been the days of my life, and
they have not reached the life spans of my forefathers
in the days of their sojourns.

(Bereishis 47:8–9)

According to *Daas Zekenim*, *Baalei HaTosafos*, Pharaoh asked Yaakov how old he was because Yaakov looked
much older than his age. According to the midrash, Yaakov
then explained that the pain and stress he had experienced
from the trials of Dina's abduction and Yosef's presumed
death had aged him. Since this took the form of a complaint
against God, moreover a complaint made before a monarch
who not only did not believe in Yisrael's God, but thought of
himself as a God in his own right, this statement constituted
lashon hara against Hashem.

As punishment for this, Yaakov lived only 147 years, in
contrast to his father Yitzchak, who lived until 180. From this
we learn that the punishment for speaking *lashon hara* can
be having what we complained about as "not good enough"
taken away from us altogether — in this case, the years of
one's life. Although the comment was not made on Yaakov's
own initiative — it was the answer to a question posed to
him — we have to remember that we are responsible for

speaking *lashon hara* even when others purposely or inadvertently prod us into it. This is a very common pitfall encountered on the road to pure speech.

Yet another point related to *shemiras halashon* can be found in the above interchange. When Yaakov was asked how old he was, why didn't he simply answer "a hundred and thirty years"? Rabbi Avraham Korman, in his book *Avot Ushevatim*, offers an explanation. The ancient Egyptians had a different system of marking the passage of time than other cultures. It would have been meaningless to Pharaoh had Yaakov simply told him how old he was. By stating that his forefathers had lived longer and he had not yet reached their age, he had put his answer in a more understandable context. This demonstrates that when we speak to people who have a different frame of reference than ours, we have to be careful to make ourselves clear so that we won't be misunderstood. If Yaakov Avinu were alive today, he would surely be considered a phenomenon not only because of his high level of spirituality but because of his age, yet he didn't live as long as his forefathers had.

The Jewish people have always marked the passage of time according to the Jewish calendar but because most of the Western world keeps the Gregorian calendar, we are frequently called upon to use their dates. We must learn from Yaakov Avinu to always keep the other person's frame of reference in mind. That will help prevent misunderstandings and *lashon hara*.

Parashas

Vayechi

I n the book *Listen to Your Messages,* by Rabbi Yissocher Frand (Artscroll), Rabbi Frand relates that on the wall in Kever Rachel there is a prayer that asks God to help us see the good in everyone (the prayer is quoted at the end of this book, "Prayer for Judging Favorably"). Why specifically this prayer?

Rav Yaakov Lubin gives the following explanation: Kever Rachel represents the idea of giving the benefit of the doubt. Rashi writes that when Yaakov Avinu asked Yosef to bring him to Israel for burial, he opened an old wound. Yosef always resented his father for the fact that he buried his mother on the side of the road. All these years, Yaakov didn't find a need to justify his behavior to his young son but now that he wanted a favor, he felt obliged to tell him.

God wanted him to bury her there because a thousand years later, when the nation would be exiled to Babylonia, they would pass by her grave and she would pray for them: "Rachel weeps for her children" (*Yirmeyahu* 31:14). Yosef couldn't have known the reason except through *ruach hakodesh*. But in any case, there was a reason. He should have given his father the benefit of the doubt. It all goes back to the same matter. Whatever we see or think we see, it's only the tip of the iceberg, the tip that is above the surface.

What about the iceberg below the surface? Are there other details to the story? Are there other sides to the episode we are judging? Are there perhaps mitigating circumstances, explanations which we couldn't imagine? We have no way of knowing. One thing is clear, though, we can't judge an iceberg by its tip.

When Yaakov blesses Yosef, he says:

They embittered him and became antagonists; the arrow-tongued men hated him. But his bow was firmly emplaced and his arms were gilded, from the hands of

the Mighty Power of Yaakov — from there, he shep-
herded the stone of Yisrael.

(Bereishis 49:23–24)

According to Rashi, these two verses are linked: Yosef
rose to great stature despite being the object of much hate
and scorn and having suffered at the hands of his brothers
and his future mother-in-law. People with arrow-like tongues
— a Scriptural allusion to purveyors of malicious slander
and gossip — dealt bitterly with Yosef, but by the grace of
God, he rose to prominence despite them.

People often (more often than not) spread gossip and
slander out of jealousy, with either a conscious or uncon-
scious hope of thwarting the success of people whom they
consider unworthy of success. But God is the One who de-
termines someone's success, and those who are worthy in
God's eyes will succeed, as did Yosef, despite the plots of
others to undermine them. Not only will they succeed, but
the people who spoke against them will have their words and
plots of slander come back to haunt them as Yosef's brothers did: the brothers feared Yosef's vengeance after their father's death so much that they claimed their father asked
that Yosef do nothing to harm them, even though Yaakov

had never made such a request. And when Potiphar ended up giving his daughter as a bride to Yosef, it only went to prove the irony of his previous claim that Yosef had tried to seduce his wife.

When we speak ill of others in the hope that we will bring about their downfall, we more often than not thwart ourselves instead. And those destined for greatness will arrive there despite our efforts to throw them off track.

Shemos

Moshe Rabbeinu would ask himself, why were *b'nei Yisrael* enslaved over the other nations...they spoke *lashon hara* among themselves so how could they be worthy of redemption?

(Midrash Rabbah, Rashi on Shemos 2:14)

Parashas

Shemos

The book of *Shemos* begins "And these are the names of the children of Israel who were coming to Egypt" (1:1) — but we already had the list of *b'nei Yisrael* who descended into Egypt, two *parashios* ago. Why does the Torah repeat it here?

A person's name, his reputation, is very important. According to Kabbalah, a person's essence is connected to his name. Therefore, *b'nei Yisrael* didn't change their names when they lived in Egypt, which is one of the reasons given for their being worthy of redemption.

> A new king arose over Egypt, who did not know of Yosef.
>
> *(Shemos 1:8)*

We can understand this phrase in a number of ways. He

didn't know Yosef; or Yosef's good name and his reputation no longer influenced Pharaoh's house. But in Pharaoh's palace, Yosef wasn't called Yosef, rather *Tzafnat Pane'ach*. Therefore his essence as an Ivri no longer influenced the decisions of Pharaoh's house regarding *b'nei Yisrael*.

As soon as we lose our good name, we are enslaved. Therefore it is extremely important not to hurt someone's good name. As soon as someone loses his good name, he goes from being a free man to a slave of *lashon hara*.

> Moshe was frightened and he thought, "Indeed, the matter is known!"
>
> *(Shemos 2:14)*

In the plain meaning, it was no longer a secret that Moshe had killed the Egyptian attacker. According to the midrash (Rashi), Moshe now understood why the Jews deserved to suffer so: They quarreled and carried tales about one another.

> Pharaoh heard about the matter and sought to kill Moshe.
>
> *(Shemos 2:15)*

According to Rashi, Pharaoh heard because someone

told him. It doesn't say that Pharaoh investigated the matter or that he discussed it with Moshe, only that he decided to kill him on the basis of a rumor. If a prince of Egypt could incur the death sentence on the basis of hearsay, how much more so is gossip dangerous to the average person? This episode also demonstrates the moral inferiority of the nations of the world whose monarchs are prepared to put to death members of the royal family at the instigation of hearsay. Is the world any better today, where leaders are judged based on stories printed about them in the newspapers and tabloids?

The Baal Shem Tov says that a person cannot see evil in others if he doesn't possess a spark of it himself. This is shown to be true later in the parashah when God tells Moshe to go and free the Jewish people. One of the reasons he objected was that "they will not believe me and they will not heed my voice, for they will say, 'Hashem did not appear to you' " (*Shemos* 4:1). According to Rashi, the sign of *tzaraas*, given by God to Moshe, was also a punishment for the *lashon hara* Moshe spoke in assuming the people would not believe him. According to Ramban, both signs, the snake and *tzaraas*, were to show him that like the snake in Eden, he had spoken slander against the Jews. Therefore, the reason Moshe recognized and was the victim of *lashon hara* was that he was capable of it himself.

When we criticize others, we must realize that we possess the same faults we see in them and must work to correct them in ourselves. The subconscious reason we may speak *lashon hara* about faults in others is to distract people's attention from our own faults by disparaging others with the same tendencies. But this tactic is rarely successful.

In Rabbi Mordechai Kamenetzky's book *Parashah Parables*, he points out that the enslavement of the Jews was brought about through *lashon hara*. Even though up until that point, *b'nei Yisrael* had been model citizens, the Egyptians started a rumor that if war were to break out, the nation might turn against them. This had no basis in truth and was a clear case of *motzi shem ra*. Pharaoh and his advisors then acted upon that assumption, and the rest is a bitter lesson about what can happen when you spread malicious slander. Not only did the Jewish people suffer, but through this, the Egyptians brought about the collapse of their own empire and the downfall of their ruler in view of the whole world.

Parashas

Va'eira

Chazal say that we can learn something from every nation of the world. We definitely can learn something from Pharaoh. Someone who truly believes in something will not be convinced to the contrary regardless of the amount of conflicting evidence. Pharaoh believed himself to be omnipotent and didn't believe in God. No matter what proofs were brought before him, no matter what rained down on him — locusts or hail — he didn't budge from his beliefs.

We are not very different from Pharaoh. If we believe something, it is difficult to convince us that it isn't true. Therefore we must be very careful regarding what we accept as truth or allow others to believe is true, because the moment that some idea becomes part of our belief system, even the plagues of Egypt can't eradicate it from our memory. We must try to keep an open mind and not jump to con-clusions about things we hear or see. Otherwise we will be living in perpetual darkness.

Parashas

Bo

So that Hashem's Torah may be in your mouth...
(Shemos 13:9)

I n this parashah there is the mitzvah of "and you shall tell your son" (*Shemos* 13:8).

The purpose of the Oral Law was to keep it oral. Jewish liturgy is full of *aggadah* and *haggadah*, the root of both being "to tell," as they were meant to be told and related from one generation to the next. Jews try to learn as much of the sacred texts as they can by heart: *tehillim, mishnayos, masechtos*. For two thousand years, this ability has served as one of the tools for religious survival, because a Jew was never sure when his holy books would be confiscated or burned, or when he would have to flee for his life with only the shirt on his back. We are a people whose mouths are constantly moving in prayer, in learning, and in benediction. So how do we still find time to speak *lashon hara*?

God gave us so much to do with our mouths. On a winter's day, the days are short. We get up, daven *shacharis*, bless the food and eat it, say the grace after meals. In the middle of the meal, it starts to rain. All of a sudden there's thunder and lightening and we have to make a *berachah*. After the meal, we notice a rainbow, "*Baruch zocher habris*." *Minchah* is recited early, we have a *shiur, ma'ariv*, women gather to say *tehillim*. The children need help with their Torah homework, we say Shema with the kids before they go to sleep. When, exactly, do we have time to talk *lashon hara*? How? Aren't our jaws tired? Wouldn't our tongues like to just rest in their palates a minute? We are always just before a blessing, "How are you?" "*Baruch Hashem!*" We are any minute awaiting salvation, "*Be'ezras Hashem*." Let's wait with God's Torah in our mouths and His blessings on our lips, and let's not forget to tell our children.

Pesach received its name because God passed over the homes of the Israelites. It is said in the name of the Arizal that the word "Pesach" is also an allusion to the Haggadah — *peh sach*, "the mouth speaks" and tells the story of

Pesach. When we tell a story, our mouths speak — *peh sach* — and there are details that we can pass over — *pesach* — and thereby not fall into the trap of *lashon hara*.

The month of Nissan is the month of miracles. The difference in *gematria* between Nissan and *nissim* is ten. *Nissim*/miracles + the ten plagues = the month of Nissan. One of the miracles is that after *b'nei Yisrael* descended to the forty-ninth level of impurity they rose to the forty-ninth level of spirituality before receiving the Torah. That's a transcendence of ninety-eight spiritual levels!

We sometimes also descend in our level of spirituality following a difficult *nissayon*. Notice that "*nissayon*" also includes the letters of "Nissan," which is the month of *nissyonot* (trials).

Shemiras Halashon is a *nissayon* that we are always facing. Each time we succeed in guarding our tongues, we raise our spiritual level and bring miracles to the world. Each one of us is supposed to see ourselves as if we have left Egypt. We are each capable of raising our spiritual level by guarding our speech.

Parashas

Beshalach

Shabbos Shirah

It was told to the king of Egypt that the people had fled.
(Shemos 14:5)

How's that? In the previous parashah, Pharaoh himself said that they could go. This parashah begins with "It happened when Pharaoh sent out the people" (*Shemos* 13:17). According to Rashi, Pharaoh sent out spies to go with the Jews to see if they would return at the end of three days, and when they didn't return, the spies came and told Pharaoh that they weren't coming back. Whatever the explanation for Pharaoh's amnesia, this clearly illustrates the power of *lashon hara*. All it takes is someone to arouse our anger, and we can forget our promises, our decisions, even the torment of a year of plagues.

It appears that the Jews also have selective amnesia.

Over and over again they complained to Moshe, and again and again they saw the salvation of God. It seems a little odd that, with every step, they renewed their complaints. How is it that the Jewish people didn't have faith in God to save them from Pharaoh and provide them with food and water after all the miracles He had performed for them?

Memory is an important tool in refraining from speaking *lashon hara*. During *Shabbos Shirah*, we remember the birds that didn't eat the manna that fell in the desert. If we are meant to remember the good turn done to us by the birds 3,000 years ago, surely we are meant to remember the kind deeds, the favors, and the gestures which our friends, neighbors, and family members perform for us daily, and judge them favorably. If we succeed in that, then we can all sing.

Parashas
Yisro

Yisro, the minister of Midian, the father-in-law of Moshe, heard everything that God did to Moshe and Yisrael His people" (*Shemos* 18:1). And Yisro took Tzipporah and her sons and went to meet Moshe in the desert. Then, "Moshe told his father-in-law everything that Hashem had done" (18:8). The question arises, if Yisro had already heard, why did Moshe have to tell him again? And why only after Yisro speaks to Moshe does he say, "Now I know that Hashem is greater than all the Gods" (18:11)? Then he goes to offer a sacrifice. Why did he wait?

I believe that Yisro acted wisely. Although he had heard of the miracles that were performed for the people, he hadn't heard about them firsthand. Only after he heard everything from Moshe's lips could he believe that he heard the whole truth, and then He could praise God and offer sacrifices.

How often do we hear stories which at their core might be true but have gone through some alteration, exaggeration, addition, subtraction, etc.? We need to verify the facts of any story we hear at its source before we react, even positively. If you hear that someone is expecting a baby and you go to congratulate her, or that someone got engaged, or has a new job, and it turns out you were wrong, it could turn your congratulations into *ona'as devarim* (words that inflict pain). It goes without saying that we shouldn't believe anything negative.

> You shall not bear false witness against your fellow.
>
> *(Shemos 20:13)*

A false witness isn't necessarily someone who lies deliberately. It could just be someone who thinks he knows the story but didn't verify it in enough depth. He passes on his version of the events without finding out the facts firsthand. According to Sforno, this commandment prohibits gossip and slander as well as bearing false witness. The Sages apply it to prohibit testimony even in cases where a witness is convinced that something took place but did not actually witness it himself. For example, if someone's scrupulously honest teachers or friends told him about something, he may not claim to be a witness to it (*Shavuos* 31a).

If Yisro could travel such a long way to speak to Moshe and verify the facts before he did something positive like praise Hashem, we too can at least pick up the phone and check that what we heard in fact happened the way we heard it. Then we won't spread *lashon hara*, which, for the most part, is also bearing false witness.

Parashas

Mishpatim

In *parashas Mishpatim*, the Torah speaks of the responsibility we have towards people whom we have hurt, either deliberately or by accident, and the ways in which we can repair the damage. But when we speak *lashon hara*, there isn't any way to repair the damage — not with money, not through medical intervention, not through indenture. The damage has been done and we are responsible.

The parashah discusses the sensitivity we have to show to people who may be vulnerable: the convert, the orphan, the widow, and the slave. *Rachmanus* (compassion) is one of the three qualities, along with modesty and *chesed*, that characterize the Jewish people. There are many halachos that require us to show compassion even to animals, *kal vachomer* people.

Whoever guards himself from speaking *lashon hara* can count himself among the compassionate of Israel and innocent before the Heavenly Court.

Parashas

Terumah

I n *parashas Terumah*, God requests contributions for the Mishkan. He says, "From every man whose heart motivates him you shall take My portion" (*Shemos* 25:1). Everyone gives according to his heart. Then God explains what kind of contribution he wants: gold, silver, and copper; and turquoise, purple, and scarlet wool, etc. The things included in the list have great value — gold, silver, oil, jewels. In other words, anyone can contribute what they want, no one is obligated. But if they are already contributing, the contribution must have value.

It's the same regarding speech. No one needs to speak if he doesn't want to. However, if somebody does contribute to a conversation, it has to be something of value, something that contributes to the service of God. There is no place for *lashon hara* or gossip in the service of God. Our words must be pure, positive, for the sake of Heaven. For God says, "They shall make a Sanctuary for Me — so that I may dwell among them" (*Shemos* 25:8).

Tetzaveh

A gold bell and a pomegranate, a gold bell and a pomegranate on the hem of the robe all around. It must be on Aharon in order to minister. Its sound shall be heard when he enters the Sanctuary before Hashem and when he leaves so that he not die.

(Shemos 28:34–35)

I n *Erchin* 16a on *Shemos* 28, there is a *gemara* that the robe of the *kohen gadol* atones for the sin of *lashon hara*, because God said: "Let something that makes sound come and atone for an act of sound."

Aharon had bells on his clothes. Everyone knew when he was in the vicinity. There is a halachah that someone must knock at the door before entering a room or a home, even his own home, in order not to frighten anyone or catch them at an awkward moment. Both instances have the same idea behind them — announce your presence! There are some things which people don't want to be caught in the middle of — not bad things, just things they would prefer not having other people see them doing. There are also conversations which shouldn't be suddenly interrupted. Not only because it's not pleasant for the people conversing, but because someone entering a conversation in the middle might misunderstand what is being spoken about, since they weren't there listening from the beginning. That's also true if someone just catches the last part of a conversation.

Lashon hara stems to a great extent from uncomfortable situations and overheard private conversations. Announcing our entrance into a room, a home, or a classroom prevents us from seeing things that aren't for our eyes or hearing things that aren't for our ears. Therefore, if like Aharon HaKohen we announce our presence, we not only avoid embarrassing situations, we approach Holiness.

W hen God offers to kill all of *b'nei Yisrael* and make a great nation from Moshe alone, Moshe convinces God not to do this, giving two reasons connected to *lashon hara*:

First, so that the Egyptians wouldn't say that God had freed His people only to kill them, which would be *lashon hara* about the motivation of God. His original intent had been one of compassion and love — free the people, give them the Torah, and bring them into Eretz Yisrael. Here it would look like God was cruel, Heaven forbid, not to mention how this would reflect on the nation itself — it would give a bad name to over two million people.

Why should Egypt say the following: "With evil intent did He take them out, to kill them in the mountains and to annihilate them from the face of the earth"? Relent from Your flaring anger and reconsider regarding the evil against your people.

(Shemos 32:12)

The second reason is to keep the promise God made to Avraham, Yitzchak, and Yaakov:

Remember for the sake of Avraham, Yitzchak, and Yisrael, Your servants, to whom You swore by Yourself and You told them, "I shall increase your offspring like the stars of the heaven, and this entire land of which I spoke, I shall give to your offspring, and it shall be their heritage forever."

(Shemos 32:13)

"Hashem reconsidered (*vayinachem*) regarding the evil that He declared He would do to His people" (32:14). The Hebrew word "*vayinachem*" means God was comforted. Although the sin was not yet forgiven, God's wrath was appeased. Moreover, He was comforted because He saw that Moshe wanted to avoid the more grievous sin of *lashon hara*, which, according to the Talmud, is worse than the three cardinal sins taken together: idol worship (which the people were engaged in, the sin of the Golden Calf), murder, and illicit relations (*Yerushalmi*, *Peah* 1a).

How powerful is *lashon hara* that even the thought of the *chilul Hashem* brought about by *lashon hara* was enough to appease God and to save two million people from death. Moshe could have thought of a million excuses to save the people, but he chose preventing *chilul Hashem* through *lashon hara* because he was aware of its importance, and this pleased God.

If God could overlook the sin of the Golden Calf for the sake of preventing *lashon hara* and keeping His promise, *kal vachomer* we need to conquer our own anger at the people who may have hurt and slighted us, and not speak *lashon hara* about them. We must also not use anger as an excuse not to keep our word to people. If God, Who is all-powerful, could overlook the slight to His honor by a people whom He had just freed from slavery and to whom He had given the commandments, we should be able to overlook the lesser slights done to our lesser honor by people towards whom we don't always behave a hundred percent.

Parashas
Vayakhel

I n *parashas Vayakhel*, two concepts are repeated a number of times: wise-heartedness and generosity of heart — *chachmas lev* and *nediv lev*. I believe that these two concepts are connected. Generosity of heart is wisdom. People who are generous of heart see the good in others, they aren't quick to find fault, they are giving and so can easily give the benefit of the doubt.

> Every wise-hearted person among you shall come and make everything that Hashem has commanded.
>
> *(Shemos 35:10)*

In this way, there will be unity among the people, and then the entire nation will be assembled as one.

Parashas
Pekudei

For the cloud of Hashem would be on the Tabernacle by day, and fire would be on it at night, before the eyes of all of the House of Israel throughout their journeys.

(Shemos 40:38)

B'*nei Yisrael* didn't have to believe that God was among them or to feel that He was among them — they could see it. They had signs, a cloud by day and fire by night, to remind them that God was with them on their journeys, both physical and spiritual. God is also with us on our journeys. He sees all that occurs and He hears all that is said. If we were to look at the clouds in the sky with the same awareness that *b'nei Yisrael* would look at the *anan hakavod* in the desert, we would remember that God is a witness to everything we say and it doesn't help to whisper.

We would certainly be more careful with our words.

When we finish reading each book in the Torah, we say, "*Chazak, chazak, venischazek.*" We do need to be strong and to strengthen ourselves in *shemiras halashon*.

Vayikra

Lashon hara is like a torn pillow that's hung out to dry and whose feathers scatter in the wind. Once the feathers are scattered, they can blow anywhere, and there isn't any way to retrieve them.

Parashas

Vayikra

If his offering is a feast peace-offering, if he offers it from the cattle — whether male or female — unblemished shall he offer it before Hashem.

(Vayikra 3:1–2)

The parashah speaks about *korbanos*, sacrifices. Today there aren't any *korbanos*. Today, prayer takes their place. When sacrifices were brought, the animals had to be perfect, unblemished, pure. The word used here, "*tamim*," also means innocent. Therefore our prayers too must be pure and innocent. A pure prayer cannot be uttered by the same mouth which speaks *lashon hara*, lies, words of strife, words which cause pain or embarrassment. All these are included in *lashon hara*.

"If a person will swear, expressing with his lips to do

harm or to do good" (*Vayikra* 5:4), he would have to bring a sacrifice. How can we offer up a prayer to God with the tool of a sin?

The Chafetz Chaim, *zt"l*, gave the following *mashal*: If a person wants to build a desk, he needs the proper tools, otherwise he won't be able to build a desk. When we pray or study Torah, the words that we utter each create an angel that carries our *tefillah* and Torah up to heaven. The tools we use to pray and study are our mouths. If we have used our tools to speak *lashon hara*, we have defiled and broken them and they are no longer capable of producing perfect angels fit to carry our words of prayer up to heaven. We need to preserve our tools for what they were meant for, or they will not be able to serve us properly and we will not be able to serve Hashem properly.

Each one of us brushes our teeth in the morning so that our breath is fresh and clean. In the same way that we wouldn't dream of leaving the house without brushing our teeth, except on a fast day, we also have to be careful not to leave the house without a mouth clean of *lashon hara*. May all our prayers be pure, innocent, and for a blessing.

Tzav

Moshe brought Aharon and his sons forward and immersed them in water.

(Vayikra 8:6)

The induction of Aharon and his sons into the priesthood was preceded by their immersion in a *mikvah* (Ibn Ezra and Rashi). In fact immersion in a *mikvah* is the way in which we purify ourselves after any kind of defilement or before approaching holiness. One might wonder why, in the desert and in Israel, where water is always scarce, would God command water to be used so abundantly for the purpose of spiritual purification? In fact, many times in the sojourn in the desert, the people called out for water; they were dying of thirst.

Ever notice how before people speak, they wet their

lips? If someone gives a speech there is usually a glass of water placed by his side. We can't talk if our mouths are dry. Our tongues, palates, and teeth, as well as our throats, need to be lubricated in order to function. It could be that the reason our mouths always need to be lubricated for us to be able to speak is to remind us that we must not remove the spiritual element from our speech. Our words must always be bathed in spirituality. If water has spiritually cleansing properties, and water is always present in our mouths in the form of saliva, it would seem as if we always have ideal conditions for pure speech.

At times, however, our mouths go dry. This is what happens when we talk too much, or as a result of an emotional response like anger, fear, or embarrassment, when our words come out sullied with *lashon hara*. It would be a good idea, before reacting to or partaking in a bit of "juicy gossip," to take a moment to have a drink of water and purify our speech.

Giraffes are kosher animals. They chew their cuds and have split hooves. But when was the last time you saw anyone eating a giraffe? It is rumored that the reason why Jews don't eat giraffes is that we don't know where on their long and stately necks to *shecht* them. In reality, according to Rabbi Nosson Slifkin, the impediments to *shechting* giraffes are not halachic but due to cost and practical considerations (like not enough storage space).

In any case, the fact is that *shechting* giraffes has never been a widespread custom among the Jewish people. I would like to offer a deeper explanation for this. Giraffes have the longest necks of all the animals and therefore the longest throats as well. They have enormously long tongues and big lips. Despite this — despite their very large and complex communication equipment — we never hear them. Giraffes hardly utter a sound. For all their vocal equipment, they're not very vocal. Giraffes are also the tallest animals. A giraffe can see what's going on for miles. I believe that because the giraffe is so quiet, despite her long throat, large tongue, big lips, and access to what's going on around her, as a reward, she's left alone. Although it's the *zechus* of an animal to be *shechted*, the giraffe enjoys the privilege of *arichas yamim* instead.

In my opinion, if we were to follow the giraffe's example and keep quiet in spite of our rich language, plethora of synonyms and antonyms, and ability to communicate in seventy languages, and not spread the vast reservoirs of information at our disposal, we would save ourselves from a dismal fate, as the giraffe has done. And like the giraffe, we could also reach great (spiritual) heights.

Parashas

Tazria

Whenever any of *b'nei Yisrael* were afflicted with a certain skin disease, they didn't go to the local skin doctor. They would go to the *kohen*, the spiritual leader, for a diagnosis of the disease — in other words, the spiritual level of the patient. The treatment of the patient, as well, was a spiritual procedure involving observation and purification. The Sages say that the word "*metzora*," one who is stricken with *tzara'as*, is a contraction of "*motzi ra*," one who spreads slander (*Eruchin* 15b). God rebukes his antisocial behavior by isolating him from society so that he can experience the pain he has caused others and heal through repentance.

Slowly but surely, conventional medicine is coming to the same conclusions about the spiritual nature of illness. Alternative medicine has brought to people's awareness the connection between the body, the mind, and the spirit. A naturopath who practices iridology can tell what ails someone by looking in his eyes. The truth is that the whole body, not just the eyes, bears witness to a person's emotional and spiritual state. I don't want, Heaven forbid, to imply that someone who is sick is spiritually tainted or emotionally unwell — I don't claim to know God's accounting — but it is a fact that when people have rid themselves of anger, resentment, and old hurts and have gone through some kind of psychological or spiritual cleansing, many have recovered or gone into remission from serious, even fatal illnesses.

Therefore in order to keep a healthy body and a healthy mind, we have to avoid getting angry or being resentful or jealous, and ensure we keep our mouths clean of gossip, slander, and *lashon hara*. Any doctor, alternative or conventional, checks the tongue when he examines a patient.

Metzora

The *kohen* shall command; and for the person being purified there shall be taken two live, clean birds, cedar wood, crimson thread, and hyssop.

(Vayikra 14:4)

There's a reason that birds are used in the purification ceremony. Rashi writes (*Eruchin* 16b) that chirping, twittering birds are used because the sin came about through idle twittering. The Baal HaTurim says that one bird is sent away, to signify that if the gossiper repeats his transgression the *tzara'as* will return just like a bird.

In English we say "A little birdie told me so" when we want to repeat something we've heard. A bird migrates from place to place. We can't catch it or change its course when it flies. It joins other birds and they form a flock. In the same way, one person's *lashon hara* joins another person's *lashon hara* and it forms a large entity that flies from place to place. No one can stop it or change its course.

If we're already going to imitate birds, we should coo in harmony like doves, not give a hoot about what people say about us, sing like larks, do kindness like the stork, and then we'll be as free as a bird from *lashon hara*.

Acharei Mos

Any person shall not be in the Tent of Meeting when he comes to provide atonement in the Sanctuary until his departure; he shall provide atonement for himself, for his household, and for the entire congregation of Israel.

(Vayikra 16:17)

This verse refers to the incense service which atones for the sin of *lashon hara*. According to *Chazal*, this service is performed quietly to atone for a sin that is done stealthily and behind another person's back (*Yoma* 44a). The Chofetz Chaim noted that this shows the seriousness of the sin of *lashon hara*: it's the first sin that must be atoned for before seeking forgiveness for the nation. As stated previously, when we speak *lashon hara* we are called before a heavenly tribunal and prosecuted for our sins. Therefore, *lashon hara* must be forgiven before we can seek forgiveness for our other sins.

Imagine: Yom Kippur, the holiest day of the year, and the first act of spiritual business is to atone for the most grievous sin of *lashon hara*. The seriousness of the sins relating to *lashon hara* are further illustrated in the *Al Chet* prayer, which repeats itself from the beginning of *selichos* until the end of Yom Kippur. The prayer includes no less than twelve sins out of forty-four (more than 25 percent) committed through speech:

> For the sin we've sinned before You with the utterance of the lips.
>
> For the sin we've sinned before You with harsh speech.
>
> For the sin we've sinned before You through insincere confession.
>
> For the sin we've sinned before You through foolish speech.
>
> For the sin we've sinned before You through impure lips.

For the sin we've sinned before You through denial and false promises.

For the sin we've sinned before You through evil talk.

For the sin we've sinned before You through scorning.

For the sin we've sinned before You with the idle chatter of our lips.

For the sin we've sinned before You in judgment.

For the sin we've sinned before You by gossip-mongering.

For the sin we've sinned before You through vain oath-taking.

(Artscroll Machzor for Yom Kippur)

For on this day He shall provide atonement for you to cleanse you; from all your sins before Hashem shall you be cleansed.

(Vayikra 16:30)

The *Al Chet* prayer further lists in an organized and comprehensive manner all the sins for which someone needs to ask forgiveness. One has to ask forgiveness from his fellow for any wrong he has done him over the course of the year. Regarding *lashon hara*, each person has to ask forgiveness for every instance of *lashon hara* he has spoken separately.

One can easily ease the burden of remembering every remark of *lashon hara* he made over the course of the year by carrying with him a pen and a little notebook, as do people who are trying to stick to a budget. Every time he speaks *lashon hara*, he writes down what he said, about whom it was said, and to whom he said it, and by the end of the year, he goes to everyone on the list and asks their forgiveness. Okay, so it's not that easy, and requires time and effort and discomfort, but there isn't any choice, right? Otherwise there's no way to atone for the sin. Other than refraining from *lashon hara* altogether, of course.

Parashas

Kedoshim

You shall not curse the deaf, and you shall not place a stumbling block before the blind; you shall fear your God — I am Hashem.

(Vayikra 19:14)

You shall not be a gossipmonger among your people, you shall not stand aside while your fellow's blood is shed — I am Hashem.

(Vayikra 19:16)

Whoever is a gossipmonger or speaks *lashon hara* transgresses all the sins mentioned above. Whoever speaks *lashon hara* curses the deaf, because the person about whom they're speaking cannot hear. Therefore, it is as if they are cursing the deaf. The speaker is also putting a stumbling block before the blind because he is causing the listener to transgress the prohibition of listening to *lashon hara*. The Rambam says, in *Sefer HaMitzvos*, that this verse means we are forbidden to cause someone to sin. We usually don't preface our *lashon hara* with "I'm going to speak *lashon hara* now, you interested?" and often it's too late to stop it. Whoever speaks *lashon hara* doesn't fear God, because though he'll often look around to make sure the subject of his conversation isn't around, he doesn't care that God can hear every word.

The commandment not to spill your brother's blood follows the verse about not being a gossipmonger. There's a reason for this, because someone who spreads rumors about other people can bring about his downfall and even his death.

This parashah commands us to be holy before God. It also includes the mitzvah of "You shall love your fellow as yourself" (*Vayikra* 19:18). If we love ourselves, and our neighbors, by judging everyone as righteous and not causing them to sin, only then will we really be speaking *lashon hakodesh*.

Emor

And if a man inflicts a wound in his fellow, as he did, so shall be done to him.

(Vayikra 24:19)

Whoever disparages or diminishes the value of someone else, in the end he will have the same done to him. The *Rishonim* find an allusion to this in the above verse. Besides this, in speaking *lashon hara*, he will be an object of scorn in the eyes of whoever hears him. *Chazal* say that false witnesses are held in contempt even by those who hire them (*Sanhedrin* 29a). And those who listen to them will always be wary lest one day they be the victims of their speech.

The verses which talk about what will befall someone who injures another occur within a story about someone who cursed God and was subsequently stoned to death. It's clear that this juxtaposition is not random. Whoever hurts one of God's creatures, it is as if he has blasphemed God by cursing Him. In fact, the curse in the parashah comes on the tail end of a dispute which had come to blows. If we avoid verbal disputes, they will not degenerate into physical violence, which can lead, Heaven forbid, to cursing God.

> You shall count for yourselves — from the morrow of the rest day, from the day when you bring the *omer* of the waving — seven weeks, they shall be complete.
>
> *(Vayikra 23:15)*

When counting the *omer*, if someone forgets even one day he can't continue counting with a *berachah*. We're not allowed to answer what day we're in when asked. We have to answer indirectly, "Yesterday was..." or "Tomorrow will be..." There are a great many halachos surrounding the counting of the *omer* which is a mitzvah related to speech. If we must exercise such care and caution with the mitzvah of counting the *omer*, *kal vachomer* with the rest of our utterances. If we are careful with our speech, we'll be able to begin each day with a blessing.

Parashas

Behar

If you will say: What will we eat in the seventh year? — behold! We will not sow and not gather in our crops!

(Vayikra 25:20)

We are a people who constantly worry — what will be? God takes this into account when He says that when we doubt, He will provide for us, so that there's nothing to worry about. But if we doubt God, is that not a form of *lashon hara*?

We have to fulfill our obligations towards God and not, *chalilah*, complain against Him and doubt His promises. The fact that we live every day is a miracle; the fact that we have survived so long as a nation is a miracle. We can see *hashgachah pratis* constantly, if we only look, and still we doubt God's benevolence!

God answers our question, "What will we eat in the seventh year?" — "I will ordain My blessing for you in the sixth year and I will yield a crop sufficient for the three-year period" (*Vayikra* 25:21). In other words, God will provide enough food for three years (sixth, seventh, and eighth) so that the people will not have to work the land during *shemittah*. God takes care of us despite our complaints and our doubts. Imagine what blessings we would bring upon ourselves if we were to change our complaints to words of prayer and praise!

If despite this you do not heed Me, then I shall punish you further, seven ways for your sins.

(Vayikra 26:18)

L et us imagine what would happen if every time we listened to or spoke *lashon hara*, seven people would speak *lashon hara* about us. The truth is that this is in fact what happens.

Say you tell a close friend that you saw a third friend of yours wearing a dress that didn't do much for her, and it wasn't very modest either. Your close friend goes and tells a fourth friend what you told her about your third friend, that she was wearing a really cheap and ugly dress. Number four goes to tell number five, being sure to mention your name as the person who informed number two that number three dresses like a harlot in clothes that are revolting. Not only does the gossip spread like wildfire but it gets worse every time it's repeated. And each time you're mentioned in the story, with some details thrown in about you too. Thereby you too become the object of *lashon hara*. And if it's only repeated seven times, you've gotten off easy.

The number seven, *sheva*, has the same root as the word "*lehishava*," to swear. To swear means to take complete responsibility for what you say. If we take responsibility for what we say and guard our speech, we'll avoid the multiple punishments of the transgressions committed by speaking *lashon hara*.

Bamidbar

In the *Sefer Chassidim* it's written that everyone has a certain allotment of words to use in his lifetime (besides *divrei kodesh*). A person who guards his tongue, prolongs his life.

Parashas

Bamidbar

Each one of us has a role in life. Most of us have more than one role, sometimes simultaneously. In *parashas Bamidbar*, there is a list of roles. One goes to the army, another works in the *mishkan*, one's a leader, another labors. Each according to his mission, his destiny, his age, his family. If everyone does his job, everything works fine. But if there are people who want to do a job that wasn't meant for them, or refuse to do the job they were meant to do — or worse, to criticize others about how they're doing their jobs — things don't work the way they're supposed to. It's true that there are people who try to avoid their jobs or don't do them properly. This leads to *lashon hara* or *chilul Hashem, gezel* of time and money, not enough manpower, and all kinds of other problems. Everyone has to take care to do his own job properly and not criticize how other people do theirs.

We must perform our duties properly, and when we see people who are not performing theirs the way they're supposed to, we need not criticize them but improve the way that we ourselves perform our duties. Also, it's preferable to give other people the benefit of the doubt and believe that they're performing to the best of their ability. Because they probably are.

Parashas

Naso

P arashas *Naso* contains the test of the *sotah*, a married woman who is suspected of being unfaithful to her husband. At first glance, it appears to be an awful ordeal. How humiliating, the poor woman! But actually, the opposite is the case. Every other sin or transgression is judged by a court. Judges decide whether or not somebody stole or murdered or lied. Though they have *ruach hakodesh*, or at the very least *siyata diShemaya*, they are still just human beings.

In the case of the *sotah*, it is God Himself who, through a special ceremony, demonstrates the guilt or innocence of the woman. If she is proven innocent, there is not one iota of aspersion cast at her. In contrast, when it comes to other cases, there can be complaints against the judges. In my opinion this is a *chesed* done for the woman because if she passes the test, she's vindicated and receives extra blessings.

The person who is the subject of *lashon hara* can't usually prove his innocence. First of all, he isn't formally accused of anything so he can't defend himself. Also, he often isn't even aware that people are speaking against him. Even if the *lashon hara* is proven to be false, there still remains a shadow of doubt, a tinge, a ringing in the ear, even if only subconsciously, against the person who was being spoken about. It's like having a case tried in court. Even though you're found innocent, there remains a record of your having been accused.

It would be nice if we could prove to our accusers, beyond a shadow of a doubt, that they're wrong. Nowadays, we don't have access to the ceremony of the *sotah* to clear the name of an accused woman, and without the bitter waters, her whole life can be embittered. Since the damage done is impossible to repair in most, if not all, instances of *lashon hara*, wouldn't it be better to give each other the benefit of the doubt, not spread rumors that can damage and hurt others, and not believe rumors that are already circulating? In this way, we'll always be left with a good taste in our mouths.

Parashas
Beha'aloscha

A more fitting title for this parashah might be "*Behitlonenutcha*" — when you complain. The parashah is full of complaints, of which Miriam's *lashon hara* is only the final straw. The nation complains to God that they have no meat, Moshe Rabbeinu complains to God that he can no longer carry the nation alone, Yehoshua complains against Eldad and Meidad, and in the end Miriam and Aharon complain against Moshe.

What's interesting is that God reacts differently to each complaint. Regarding the complaint of the people, first God sends fire upon them and then gives them their request, but so much so that it becomes a punishment. God grants Moshe his request but takes from him some of his *ruach hakodesh*. Miriam is punished with *tzara'as* for her *lashon hara* but Aharon isn't. Although Miriam had spoken privately with Aharon, the entire nation knows of her sin. For each incident of *lashon hara*, God responds differently.

The different times for blowing the trumpets, whether for holy work, for war, or to gather the people to continue their journey, is also mentioned in the parashah. The parashah teaches us that context makes a difference. The trumpets elicited a different response depending on the context — and God's response to the complaints and *lashon hara* differed according to the context.

It's very important that when we see or hear about someone doing something that doesn't seem right, that we not jump to conclusions until we are aware of all the circumstances surrounding the incident (which is often impossible). We are not permitted to draw conclusions about, or react to, the questionable behavior of someone else until we have looked into the matter — and truthfully, not even then. Only God is All-Knowing and only He can decide if someone acted rightly or not, according to the circumstances.

Parashas
Shelach Lecha

Miriam's sin and that of the ten out of twelve spies who were sent to spy out the land are the two most famous prototypes in the Torah of the sin of speaking *lashon hara*. There is no chronology in the Torah. So why does one follow the other? Rashi says, in order to demonstrate what happened when *b'nei Yisrael* didn't learn their lesson from Miriam's sin. Miriam spoke *lashon hara* about Moshe, in private, to right a wrong that she perceived about his treatment of his wife, Tzipporah. She was a prophetess and it was all in the family. She was then sent out of the camp for a week with *tzara'as*. The spies spoke *lashon hara* about Eretz Yisrael, in essence casting doubt on God's promise. The people accepted it and were punished by being kept out of the land for forty years.

Why did this happen? People always say, "That'll never

happen to me, I'm not like that." People aren't aware of their weaknesses. They always feel secure that what happens to their neighbor will never happen to them. They're cleverer, more careful, more righteous (or self-righteous). Things happen right in front of us for a reason. Miriam could have been sent outside the camp with a logical excuse or no reason given, but the people were told it was because of her *lashon hara*, and still they didn't learn.

Instead of talking about other people's mistakes, we have to learn from them so that we don't repeat them. As we see in the parashah, if we don't learn from other people's mistakes, the results of the ones we make are liable to be more serious.

Parashas

Korach

Korach son of Izhar son of Kohath son of Levi sepa-
rated himself...

(Bamidbar 16:1)

Pride is one of the character traits that cause the
neshamah to flee from the body. Since the
neshamah rests in the head, it causes one to lose his
mind, or at least act like he has. The fact that we're a stiff-
necked people only makes matters worse — because if
we're stiff necked, perhaps the brain doesn't get enough
oxygen.

This is the third parashah in succession that mentions
the sin of *lashon hara*. "Why aren't they getting it!?!"

The answer is that when pride controls us, there is no
place for self-control. Korach saw what happened to Miriam
when she spoke against her brother, even with good intentions and in private. He saw what happened when the spies
spoke against the land. What does he think is going to hap-

pen when he speaks against Moshe and Aharon, the leaders appointed by God, in front of the entire Assembly?

Korach has the same letters as "*kerach*," ice. Ice is frozen and its destiny is to melt. The ground swallows Korach up along with his followers. He sought to be raised up and he went lower than the ground, much like the snake in *parashas Bereishis*. The punishment is *middah keneged middah*: he wanted to prove how important he was, and in the end he was literally and figuratively swallowed up by the earth, without a trace. His only claim to fame was how unimportant he was. That's the problem with pride. Prideful people can be completely convinced that they are right and that they are only acting in the interest of the principle of the thing, of truth and justice, when the real truth is that they just want to feel important. They end up only proving how unimportant they are. The language of the conceited is *lashon hara*.

Moshe Rabbeinu fought for the truth when he came to free the nation from Egypt. At first, due to his humility, he hesitated. He only finally undertook the mission because God Himself commanded him to do so. Even then, it took a lot of convincing. Moshe Rabbeinu never sought personal glory. The proof is that he was already free. He put himself in danger by going back to free *b'nei Yisrael*.

Self-confidence is a good thing. The search for truth is a good thing. Conceit and arrogance are not. A person who isn't conceited doesn't shout his truth — he speaks it. As Shlomo HaMelech said, the words of the wise are spoken softly. Whoever isn't haughty seeks the objective truth, not only his truth. Whoever isn't haughty can succeed in his mission without deprecating others. And whoever isn't conceited will think twice before he does something that others who are on a higher spiritual level than him have failed in. At least the sons of Korach learned the lesson.

Parashas

Chukas

A fter Miriam's death, the people come once again to complain to Moshe. Three things happen here which characterize the sin of *lashon hara*:

1) The timing is very bad. Aharon and Moshe have just lost their sister. Miriam was the one who watched over Moshe in his basket in the Nile. It's thanks to Miriam that he was even born, since she was the one who convinced her father to return to her mother despite Pharaoh's evil decree against the children. "The people quarreled with Moshe" (*Bamidbar* 20:3). Wasn't it enough that Moshe was suffering because of the death of his sister? Many times we not only quarrel with people but pick the most inopportune time to do so and in the worst possible way without taking into consideration what the other person is going through at that moment.

2) Often when people complain, they bring a long list of complaints before they get to the real point of their displeasure, bringing up a whole history of dissatisfaction. "Why did you bring us up from Egypt to bring us to this evil place? — not a place of seed, or fig, or grape, or pomegranate; and there is no water to drink." The people want water, yet they preface their need with other complaints so that one comment of *lashon hara* becomes a whole barrage of it in which even a justifiable complaint gets lost.

3) It's ironic but not incidental that the species of the land of Israel are mentioned here. The people blame Moshe that they didn't go into the land despite the fact that it's their own fault or the fault of the previous generation. They have been forced to wander in the desert for forty years because they accepted the *lashon hara* of the ten spies who spoke against the land. As usual, instead of accepting responsibility for their actions, they blame Moshe by alluding to the species of the land.

It's true they didn't have water to drink. It's true they were afraid they'd die of thirst. But to choose such an inappropriate time to unburden themselves and attack Moshe, who had dedicated himself to doing everything for them, is the height of ingratitude. And after all they'd been through, the people still didn't trust God. Moshe then hit the rock in anger, instead of talking to it, and was punished with not being allowed to enter the land of Israel.

When we speak with someone, we have to pay attention to what kind of mood he's in and whether he can properly listen to what we have to say. We shouldn't add insult to injury. We also have to see where our own responsibility lies in our complaint. Maybe we've done something to warrant the other person's behavior. If we do voice what we consider a legitimate complaint, there's no need to accompany it with the vilification of every other thing that has occurred. This is especially relevant for husbands and wives and parents and children.

If we're not careful to take all of the above into consideration, we will have to share the responsibility for the consequences of our words, in the same way that the people of Israel bid their leader farewell in the desert and had to enter the land without him.

Balak

One of the main things separating us from animals is the capacity for speech. In *Parashas Balak*, God shows us that sometimes animals do talk, and they can make more sense than a human being. Therefore, we have to make an effort to demonstrate more wisdom than a talking mule. Sometimes the *yetzer hara* or the desire for revenge leads a person (or misleads him) to hurt another through *lashon hara* or, God forbid, a curse. Often, however, this person causes more damage to himself than to the intended victim, exactly like what happened to Balak.

When Bilam blessed the nation, he quoted Yitzchak's blessing in reverse. Yitzchak said, "Cursed be they who curse you and blessed be they who bless you" (*Bereishis* 27:29). Bilam said, "Those who bless you are blessed and those who curse you are accursed" (*Bamidbar* 24:9). In other words, those who wish to curse you will not succeed; only blessings will come out of their mouths. Yaakov and his progeny, the children of Israel, are protected against curses. Every curse turns into a blessing and those who try to curse them are cursed themselves.

It follows then that whoever tries to speak *lashon hara* about another person brings a curse upon himself. It is worth our while as part of the children of Israel to bring blessings upon ourselves by blessing others and not, God forbid, the opposite.

Parashas

Pinchas

There are three lessons that can be learned from this parashah that are connected to *lashon hara*.

It is written, "But the sons of Korach did not die" (*Bamidbar* 26:11), and "The daughters of Tzelafchad speak properly...you shall cause the inheritance of their father to pass over to them" (27:7). We have a tendency to think badly about people because of their parents' actions. We have two instances where it is written explicitly that the children don't have to suffer because of the sins of their fathers. Korach's sons did not join their father's rebellion, and their words of praise to God are inscribed in the book of *Tehillim*. The daughters of Tzelafchad inherited their father's land even though he died as a punishment for his sins. The message here is clear. Children don't have to get a bad name because of what their parents have done.

The daughters of Tzelafchad say: "Our father died in the wilderness, but he was not among the assembly that was gathering against Hashem in the assembly of Korach, but he died of his own sin" (*Bamidbar* 27:3). What difference does it make what sin he died from? Why even mention it? Rashi says that he died alone in his sin; he wasn't connected to Korach's rebellion and he didn't convince other people to sin. Rashi cites that Tzelafchad died because, according to Rabbi Akiva, he gathered wood on Shabbos. According to Rabbi Shimon, he was one of the *mapilim* who tried to go to Eretz Yisrael on his own (*Shabbos* 91:93).

The message here is that even if someone sins — as we are all liable to do — it is important not to exaggerate the sin or add to it. If there is a permissible reason to speak *lashon hara* — as the daughters of Tzelafchad had to talk about their father's sin in order to get their portion of the land — it's very important not to exaggerate and even to point out the positive aspect of the person. As Rashi comments, the daughters do this. They mention that their father didn't take anyone down with him. It's permissible only to stick to the pertinent facts, and it's meritorious to find merit for the sinner. So although Tzelafchad had sinned, he didn't rebel and he didn't convince others to sin with him, "but he died of his own sin."

When we want to show someone's bad character, we can do this in two ways: speak badly of him or compare him to someone who behaves better. The parashah speaks of Cozbi, daughter of Zur, who seduced Zimri, son of Salu. In contrast, the parashah also mentions the righteous women of Israel: Miriam, Yocheved, Serach, who according to the midrash encouraged Yaakov Avinu by telling him that Yosef was still alive, and the daughters of Tzelafchad who try to maintain their father's portion within the nation. It's unusual that the names of so many women are mentioned in one parashah. I believe that this comes to show us the difference between the Midianite women, who acted licentiously, and the daughters of Israel, who devoted themselves to their families and did what was right in Hashem's eyes.

The next time we want to speak badly about someone, it would be better and more constructive to praise whoever behaves properly in order to emphasize the difference. It not only achieves the same thing in a more positive way, it contributes to *kiddush Hashem*.

Parashas

Matos

The parashah begins, "If a man takes a vow to Hashem or swears an oath to establish a prohibition upon himself, he shall not desecrate his word; according to whatever comes from his mouth shall he do" (*Bamidbar* 30:3). Towards the end of the parashah, the tribes who want to remain on the other side of the Jordan River — Gad, Reuven, and half of Menashe — promise to return only after the nation is settled in the land. "What has come from your mouth shall you do" (32:24).

The parashah is framed with the concept that one must keep his word and do whatever he utters. The idea is not to lie, to be credible.

How credible are we when we speak *lashon hara*? How can we rely on the word of someone who speaks *lashon hara*? And how much of what he says is indeed true and not an exaggeration or lacking some essential detail, a mistake, or a misinterpretation? If we have to be so careful about what we say about ourselves, *kal vachomer* we should be careful regarding what we say about others. It's better to concentrate on ourselves and not speak about other people. That should keep us busy enough.

Parashas
Masei

Parashas *Masei* records the travels of the nation in the wilderness. According to Or HaChaim, God instructed Moshe to keep a "diary" of the journeys as they occurred, and now at the end of the forty years, God told him that his record was to become part of the Torah.

Many people keep diaries and journals. People allow themselves to be very honest and forthright in their personal recordings of their lives. Sometimes they exaggerate or omit things as is their right, since their journals are private, for their eyes only. Yet how many diaries have been posthumously published when the writer has no say as to whether he would have permitted its publication and can no longer edit it?

We have to be very careful about what we put in writing. We don't have God instructing us what to write like Moshe did, and we may not be around forty years from now when we might be a little more objective and discreet about what we have written. That isn't to say we can't keep journals and diaries, but even there we have to be careful of *lashon hara*. We have no way of knowing who may read the diaries after we're gone or into whose hands they might fall within our lifetime. Even if it's "only" our children who read it, we have to write in such a way that we are not speaking derogatorily about ourselves or others. At the very least we should write in a code that only we can decipher.

The fact that Moshe waited forty years before including the journeys in the Torah is a good lesson for us. Often we are anxious to express our views and opinions. We often write and send letters to the editor or letters to our friends or submit newspaper articles or reviews at the height of emotion. While that may be good for our use of figurative language, it would be wiser to wait a day or two till the issue has cooled in our minds and reread what we've written to make sure it wasn't written in the heat of the moment. If we still believe what we wrote, and we don't perceive it as unnecessarily damaging, we can always send it then.

The allocation of the cities of refuge is also discussed in

the parashah. According to the midrash, there were a disproportionate number of signs guiding anyone who sought them to the cities of refuge. The reason for this was that no one should have to ask directions, since that would reveal him as a possible killer, thereby endangering his life. We must protect people from the need to ask self-incriminating questions. Our homes must be set up in such a way that our families and guests can get whatever they need without having to be put in the uncomfortable position of asking embarrassing questions.

Devarim

עסק התורה הוא עצה שלא לבוא לידי לשון הרע .
(ערכין ט״ו)

Studying Torah is a good way to avoid forbidden speech.

Parashas

Devarim

I n this parashah, we find a paradox. "These are the words that Moshe spoke to all Yisrael" (*Devarim* 1:1). In *Shemos*, though, it is written, "Please, my Lord, I am not a man of words" (4:10).

The beginning of the book of *Devarim* is in essence a recapitulation of everything that had occurred to the nation, a kind of summary of events. So why does Moshe, who has already remarked that he is not a man of words, all of a sudden make a speech that seems superfluous? I would like to offer an explanation.

We all know that no two people experience the same event in exactly the same way. If we were to ask several people "What happened?" regarding a specific event, several similar stories would emerge but they would differ in certain details and emphasis according to the one telling the story.

When we speak of two million people, it's more than likely that there would be several versions of their experiences in the wilderness. Therefore it was important to gather the people and to repeat and clarify what had transpired in order that there be a unity of national experience. This would also eliminate many arguments that could occur after Moshe died. This job naturally fell to the leader of the people.

Similarly, when there is more than one version to a story, we must listen to all sides and clarify as much detail as possible, emphasizing what is agreed upon by all parties before we accept one person's version of a story as true. This job falls to the head of a family, the boss of a company, the chairman of a committee, or any other leader. This ensures that those for whom he is responsible understand every situation that relates to them in the most truthful and objective way possible. Furthermore, he must do this even if it is difficult for him or not his forte. In that way, God willing, there won't be any misunderstandings or *lashon hara*.

Va'eschanan

I appoint heaven and earth this day to bear witness against you.

(Devarim 4:26)

It seems a little strange that Moshe Rabbeinu uses the heaven and earth as witnesses to what he tells the children of Israel. In the first place, he is speaking in the name of God and God doesn't need witnesses to verify his words. Secondly, he is speaking in front of two million people; each person has two million other witnesses.

In order for witnesses to be completely reliable, they have to be objective. That is why Moshe chose the heaven and earth. They had no vested interest, they did not volunteer, they were chosen as being the most suitable for the job. They were not emotionally involved.

Also, they were two. In general, testimony, to be credible, has to be given by two witnesses to ensure that it isn't a product of vengeance or the self-interest of one person. Besides which, everyone sees things from his own perspective. If there are two people who see things the same way, it's more likely that they are speaking the truth. Moreover, you can't have two more diametrically opposed perspectives than heaven and earth, both in direction and in orientation. Heaven is spiritual while the earth is material. Therefore, if you want to arrive at the truth, you need two completely opposite witnesses coming from two completely different perspectives with two widely different orientations agreeing to the same thing.

When one hears *lashon hara* about someone, he generally hears it from one person who has some level of emotional involvement with the person he's speaking about or personal interest related to him. Therefore, one can't rely on what he says (except in the instances where it is permitted to do so according to halachah). If Moshe Rabbeinu, who is speaking in God's name, calls for witnesses to his words, witnesses who can't be any more opposite and objective, *kal vachomer* we are not permitted to believe the *lashon hara* which hasn't been corrobo-rated by at least two different, objective, reliable wit-nesses.

Parashas
Eikev

In this parashah, in my humble opinion, is the prototype for not accepting *lashon hara*.

> Then Hashem said to me, "Arise, descend quickly from here, for the people you took out of Egypt have become corrupt; they have strayed quickly from the way that I commanded them; they have made themselves a molten image."
>
> *(Devarim 9:12)*

Moshe responds:

> So I turned and descended from the mountain ... Then I saw and behold! You had sinned to Hashem your God... you strayed quickly from the way that Hashem commanded you. I grasped the two tablets and threw

them from my hands, and I smashed them before your eyes.

(Devarim 9:16–17)

Moshe Rabbeinu heard from God himself that *b'nei Yisrael* had sinned and made a molten image. But he didn't react to that until he had witnessed it for himself, "I turned… I saw… and threw."

Beis Elokim says that this comes to teach us that even though Hashem doesn't, *chalilah,* speak *lashon hara,* and Moshe didn't doubt what He told him, Moshe had to see it for himself. In the same way that we learn a great lesson in *hachnasas orchim* from Avraham Avinu, who turned away from his conversation with God to welcome guests, we can similarly learn from Moshe how not to accept *lashon hara* until we see something with our own eyes.

If we hear someone saying something negative about someone else, we have to behave as Moshe did. We must turn away from the conversation, not accept what we hear until we see it for ourselves, and only then, react accordingly.

Moshe uses the exact same terminology that God does when he says that *b'nei Yisrael* had "strayed quickly from the way that Hashem commanded you." He uses the same words to show that each word that God had spoken was true. They had strayed, and done so quickly, from the path that God had commanded them. This attention to choice of words would be best learned by ourselves, who often add commentary, exaggerate, or use more figurative language when describing an event.

In *parashas Ki Sisa*, which relates the same incident, it says that "Moshe pleaded before God... Relent from Your flaring anger and reconsider..." (*Shemos* 32:12). Even there, Moshe answers in general terms and doesn't directly relate to the "alleged" sin of the people. He then tries to calm God down. We should do likewise and try to appease the anger of those who speak in anger about others.

Therefore, even if the most reliable person that we know tells us anything that resembles *lashon hara*, it is forbidden for us to listen to it, accept it, or respond to it until we've checked out that things are exactly as he said.

If in one of your cities that Hashem your God gives you in which to dwell, you hear it said, "Lawless men have emerged from your midst..." you shall seek out and investigate and inquire well and behold! It is true, the word is correct, this abomination was committed in your midst.

(Devarim 13:13–15)

Acc, ording to Rashi, the report of "lawless men" can't just be said, it has to be said by witnesses who give testimony in court. The Sages derive from the nuances of the verse that the instigators must be men, citizens of that town, who are accused of carrying their campaign out to groups of people rather than to individuals.

There are three things which must be done: seek out,

investigate, and inquire well. Rashi understands from this that we must ask the person to pinpoint the crime in seven ways, including month, day, year of *shemittah*, time, place, and nature of the crime. Then, according to Rambam (*Hilchos Avodah Zarah* 4:5) they have to verify that the idolatry was actually committed, not just agitated or suggested.

Rambam rules that after the court has established that most of the city is guilty, it sends two Torah scholars there to try and influence the people to repent. If they succeed and the people repent, the city is not treated as a wayward city that must be completely destroyed. Ralbag finds support for Rambam's ruling, because if they have repented, it is in effect no longer the same city. In the same way, a person who becomes a *ba'al teshuvah* is considered to have been reborn.

L'havdil, how well do we investigate when we hear someone is trying to cause someone else to leave the right path or do something wrong? How often do we condemn them without even checking it out, let alone interrogating witnesses in court, asking seven times, or making sure that the person is really privy to the information? How often do we hear something negative about someone and are quick to not only believe it but pass it on (with the best of intentions to warn others).

In the parashah God speaks of *avodah zarah*, which is a very serious sin. Rashi says that as long as there is idolatry in the world, there is Divine anger in the world. Since *lashon hara* is considered worse than idolatry, how much more must we be careful of making or believing accusations.

Parashas
Shoftim

And it will be told to you and you will hear…

(Devarim 17:4)

The above *pasuk* and the ones following repeat the caution to investigate an accusation well before passing judgment. What is also repeated is "and you will hear": only if you happen to be told about it and you hear. In other words, accept only things you hear directly and not secondhand; accept only words to which you were paying attention and listening carefully, not things you heard by eavesdropping on someone else's conversation or only partially heard.

Many of us go looking for trouble — that is, the trouble that other people are in. We're always on the lookout for a "good story" like hardened journalists who try to sniff out a lead, but not for some higher purpose. If you try to avoid this attitude, but nevertheless a sin comes to your attention, then investigate it well. It is forbidden to seek out the bad in the next person for anything but a constructive purpose.

During the time of the Sanhedrin, a court that put to death one person in seventy years was considered cruel. How much more cruel are we that we murder people through slander on a regular basis.

Ki Seitzei

On *Shabbos Zachor* we read "Remember what Amalek did to you, on the way, when you were leaving Egypt" (*Devarim* 25:17). Earlier in *parashas Ki Seitzei*, it's written: "Remember what Hashem, your God, did to Miriam on the way, when you were leaving Egypt" (24:9).

The language is identical. And we know that when there is similar or identical language, there's a reason. What's the connection? "Amalek came and battled Israel in Rephidim" (*Shemos* 17:8), and "...He struck those of you who were hindmost, all the weaklings at the rear, when you were faint and exhausted" (*Devarim* 25:18). Amalek didn't attack the soldiers and strong among *Am Yisrael*, but the weak and vulnerable. The interpretation refers to the spiritually weak.

What God did to Miriam was as a result of the *lashon hara* that she spoke about her brother. When we speak *lashon hara*, we attack the weak points (real and imagined) of the other person, where he's vulnerable. Therefore the punishment, leprosy, is *middah keneged middah*. It's an illness which weakens the body, brings about wounds, and reduces its victim to a vulnerable state. The mitzvah of wiping out Amalek also relates to wiping out *lashon hara* and any behavior which attacks a vulnerable person. When we strive to wipe out the sin of *lashon hara*, we are also wiping out the memory of Amalek.

Lashon hara is prevalent in the story of Purim. The evil Haman, a descendent of Amalek, was angry with Mordechai and therefore told Achashverosh that the Jews don't listen to the king and must all be killed, even the weak, old, and infirm. He slandered the Jews and almost succeeded in destroying them, only to further his own interests. Yet he presented his plot as if it were for the sole purpose of increasing the honor of the king.

In contrast, Mordechai saved the life of the king by exposing Bigtan and Teresh's plot to kill him. He had no interest in furthering his own career at the palace, only in protecting the king. In the end, his warning was not only instrumental in protecting Achashverosh, but in saving the entire Jewish people from Haman' s machinations. Also, because his motives were devoid of self-interest, he merited to take Haman's place in the palace.

We all have the choice of being like Haman or like Mordechai in the way we speak — to invent evil stories about other people to serve our own interests or only to tell the truth when necessary to expose something that could prove harmful to someone else. The question is whose honor are we protecting? And who will be sacrificed to it?

> If a man marries a wife and comes to her and hates her, and he makes a wanton accusation against her, spreading a bad name against her...
>
> *(Devarim 22:13–14)*

In this verse, a husband gives his wife a bad name in order to end his marriage and not pay her *kesubah*. According to Rashi, one sin brings another in its wake. A man who sins by hating will come to commit slander.

In general, whoever slanders another person has some personal interest in harming the other person. If they have no such interest, it's worse because they're doing it for no other reason than to be malicious.

Once again, the fact that *shemiras halashon* is mentioned several times in the parashah only underscores its importance.

Then we cried out to Hashem, the God of our forefathers, and Hashem heard our voice.

(Devarim 26:7)

When something bothers us, it weighs heavily on our hearts, and we feel the need to complain about it to someone, even when it involves someone else and *lashon hara*. For this, the Torah offers a solution to avoid speaking *lashon hara*: simply cry out to Hashem and complain to Him. If we turn to Him instead of spreading *lashon hara*, then Hashem will hear our voice. He's the only one who can help in any case.

"Accursed is one who strikes his fellow stealthily." And the entire people shall say, "Amen."

(Devarim 27:24)

To speak *lashon hara* is to strike one's fellow stealthily. Many times *lashon hara* about someone is circulated and the person being spoken about doesn't know who the source of the gossip is, how it started, and who's spreading it onwards. Like in journalism, the source isn't revealed. We must save ourselves from the curse of a person who stabs someone in the back by speaking *lashon hara* about him, and let the entire congregation say Amen.

Parashas

Nitzavim

The hidden [sins] are for Hashem, our God, but the revealed [sins] are for us and our children...

(Devarim 29:28)

We never know the whole truth about the reasons behind someone's behavior, why he acts a certain way, what motivates him, what he's thinking, what the aim of his actions is. Nevertheless we judge him, and even add our own interpretations of his motivations when we reveal our insights to others.

Only God can judge a person's behavior because only He knows the whole story and the circumstances behind anyone's actions. He knows what thoughts and goals and feelings are behind every action and what someone's true intentions are, which are often the exact opposite of what they appear to be. We cannot draw conclusions about a person based on what is observable to us, and most people don't investigate further — though further investigation would still not reveal the complete picture.

Therefore we are obligated to give the benefit of the doubt when we see someone acting in an apparently unacceptable way and to realize that in most cases, we haven't got the faintest idea what is going on behind the scenes.

Parashas
Vayeilech

Moshe summoned Yehoshua and said to him before the eyes of all Yisrael, "Be strong and courageous, for you shall come with this people to the land that Hashem swore to their forefathers to give them, and you shall cause them to inherit it."

(Devarim 31:7–8)

Many people, from company bosses to parents, turn authority over to others when they can't be available themselves. The only trouble is they usually tell their subordinates whom they elect to be in charge but not the people whom they are charging to their care. That often leads to ill feelings and jealousy. When Moshe turned over leadership to Yehoshua in front of the whole nation, there could be no doubt as to who was now the new leader of

Israel, thereby averting any kind of rebellion or uncertainty.

Inasmuch as rebuke or negative speech should take place in private, praise and designation of authority should take place in public when appropriate, so that there is no misunderstanding or chance of bitterness (unless this will cause more jealousy or ill-feeling than it will prevent). We should always make sure we delegate authority and clarify who's in charge before the people who are to be taken care of, whether it's our young children or a department of a corporation, so that there is no name-calling or backstabbing or reports of insubordination.

Parashas
Ha'azinu

Give ear, O heavens, and I will speak; and may the earth hear the words of my mouth…when I call out the name of Hashem, ascribe greatness to our God.

(Devarim 32:1–3)

Ask your father and he will relate it to you, your elders and they will tell you.

(Devarim 32:7)

In *parashas Ha'azinu* we are encouraged to speak and to listen, but what we are encouraged to speak about and listen to is the greatness of God. When was the last time we were at a party or in the park or even at the Shabbos table and spoke about the wonders of Creation, the greatness of God, or some miracle that happened to us this week (and miracles happen to us daily)? When did we last speak about how beautiful the weather is (as opposed to complaining about it) or even the serendipity of events?

When people are told not to speak *lashon hara*, they usually ask, "So what can we talk about?" The answer can be found in *parashas Ha'azinu*. We are to speak about the greatness of God, we are to ask our parents and elders questions, and listen when they speak about God's infinite benevolence. We have to educate our children to speak of God's greatness on a daily basis. There's a lot to say on the subject. So much, in fact, that there is no need to talk about anything else, *kal vachomer, lashon hara*.

Parashas
Vezos Haberachah

So Moshe, servant of Hashem, died there, in the land of Moav, by the mouth of Hashem.

(Devarim 34:5)

The intention in the above verse is to indicate that Moshe died by a Divine kiss. But ordinary people can die, God forbid, by the mouths of regular people and not by a kiss. I have read many true stories where people have been caused such grief and misfortune through slander and gossip — resulting in their losing a job or a *shidduch* — that it even led to their early demise. In times of war, spies and betrayers have sent people to their deaths with their mouths. The capacity for good or evil inherent in speech is great and powerful. As soon as we liberate information, whether true or false, we lose all control over it and we have no way of knowing to what it may lead.

> Go and discern which is the proper way to which a man should cling...Rabbi Shimon says: One who considers the outcome of a deed.
>
> *(Pirkei Avos 2:13)*

It's imperative to consider the consequences of everything we do and say. It's critical that we consider a hundred times before we speak about someone else — because in this case, the person who considers the outcome of a deed may prevent a tragedy, even death.

Again we say, "*Chazak, chazak, venitchazek.*" We should become strong. We should strengthen our determination to refrain from speaking or listening to *lashon hara* and this will give us the strength we need to succeed in all other areas of our lives.

May God bless our efforts to guard our speech and our relationships, and may all *klal Yisrael* reap the benefits of *shemiras halashon.*

Special Prayers

The Prayer for Shemiras HaLashon

רִבּוֹנוֹ שֶׁל עוֹלָם, יְהִי רָצוֹן מִלְּפָנֶיךָ, קֵל רַחוּם
וְחַנּוּן, שֶׁתְּזַכֵּנִי הַיּוֹם וּבְכָל יוֹם לִשְׁמוֹר אֶת עַצְמִי
מִלְּסַפֵּר וּלְקַבֵּל לָשׁוֹן-הָרָע וּרְכִילוּת.
וְאֶזָּהֵר מִלְּדַבֵּר אֲפִלּוּ עַל אִישׁ יְחִידִי, וְכָל שֶׁכֵּן
מִלְּדַבֵּר עַל כְּלַל יִשְׂרָאֵל, וְכָל שֶׁכֵּן מִלְּהִתְרָעֵם עַל
מִדּוֹתָיו שֶׁל הַקָּדוֹשׁ-בָּרוּךְ הוּא.
וְאֶזָּהֵר מִלְּדַבֵּר דִּבְרֵי שֶׁקֶר, חֲנֻפָּה, לֵצָנוּת,
אוֹנָאַת דְּבָרִים, הַלְבָּנַת פָּנִים, גַּאֲוָה, מַחֲלֹקֶת,
כַּעַס, וְכָל דִּבּוּרִים אֲסוּרִים.
וְזַכֵּנִי שֶׁלֹּא לְדַבֵּר כִּי אִם דָּבָר הַצָּרִיךְ לְעִנְיְנֵי
גוּפִי וְנַפְשִׁי, וְשֶׁיִּהְיוּ כָּל מַעֲשַׂי וְדִבּוּרַי לְשֵׁם שָׁמַיִם.

Master of the Universe, may it be Your will, Merciful and Gracious God, that I merit today and every day to guard myself from relating and accepting *lashon hara* and *rechilus*.

May I be careful not to speak even about one individual, and all the more so about the nation of Israel, and all the more so about the actions of *HaKadosh Baruch Hu*.

May I be careful not to speak words of falsehood, flattery, mockery, hurtfulness, humiliation, arrogance, controversy, anger, and all other forbidden speech.

May I merit to speak only words that are necessary for my body and my soul, and may all my actions and words be for the sake of Heaven.

Excerpted from sefer Chafetz Chaim

Prayer for Judging Favorably

יְהִי רָצוֹן מִלְפָנֶיךָ ד׳ אֱלֹקֵי וֵאלֹקֵי אֲבוֹתַי שֶׁתַּעַזְרֵנִי
בְּרַחֲמֶיךָ וְתַדְרִיכֵנִי וְתוֹרֵנִי דֶרֶךְ יְשָׁרָה בְּאוֹפֶן
שֶׁאֶזְכֶּה לִשְׁמֹר עַצְמִי בְּרַחֲמֶיךָ שֶׁלֹּא אֶכָּשֵׁל בְּשׁוּם
דָּבָר שֶׁאֵינוֹ טוֹב וְלֹא אוֹמֵר דָּבָר שֶׁלֹּא כִרְצוֹנֶךָ
וְתִזַכֵּינִי לִהְיוֹת טוֹב לַכֹּל תָּמִיד וְלֹא אֶחְקֹר לְעוֹלָם
אַחַר חוֹבוֹת בְּנֵי אָדָם חַס וְשָׁלוֹם.

רַק אַדְרַבָּה, אֶזְכֶּה לְהִשְׁתַּדֵּל תָּמִיד בְּכָל כֹּחַ וָעֹז
וּגְבוּרָה לִמְצֹא תָּמִיד זְכוּת וְטוֹב בְּכָל אֶחָד וְאֶחָד
מִבְּנֵי יִשְׂרָאֵל עַמְּךָ הַקָּדוֹשׁ אֲפִילוּ בַּפְּחוֹת
שֶׁבַּפְחוּתִים וַאֲפִילוּ בַּקַל שֶׁבַּקַּלִּים, אֲפִילוּ
בְּלוֹחֲמִים וְהָרוֹדְפִים אוֹתִי כּוּלָם אֶזְכֶּה בְּרַחֲמֶיךָ
לְדוּנָם לְכַף זְכוּת תָּמִיד. וְתִתֶּן לִי שֵׂכֶל לָדַעַת
מֵאִתְּךָ אֵיךְ לְחַפֵּשׂ וְלִמְצֹא בָּהֶם זְכוּת וּנְקוּדוֹת
טוֹבוֹת תָּמִיד.

May it be your will Hashem, my God and the God of my forefathers, that You should assist me in Your mercy, guide me and show me the straight path so that I will safeguard myself in Your mercy, not to stumble in anything not good and not to speak anything which is not in accordance with Your will. May I merit always to be good to everyone and that I should not find faults in anyone, Heaven forfend.

Rather, may I always be worthy to do my utmost, using all my capabilities to find merit and worth in each and every member of the Jewish people, Your holy nation, even the smallest of the small and even those who stand up against me. Through Your mercy, may I always merit to judge others favorably; may You bestow upon me the intelligence to understand how to search for and find redeeming factors, strengths, and virtues in my fellowman at all times.

The Chofetz Chaim Heritage Foundation. Translation from
The Other Side of the Story by Reb. Yehudis Samet,
with permission from Mesorah Publications

A *segulah* for not speaking *lashon hara*
is to say Tehillim 52.

From the Prayer of
Rav Elimelech of Lizhensk

אַדְרַבָּה, תֵּן בְּלִבֵּנוּ שֶׁנִּרְאֶה כָּל אֶחָד מַעֲלוֹת
חֲבֵרֵינוּ, וְלֹא חֶסְרוֹנָם, וְשֶׁנְּדַבֵּר כָּל אֶחָד אֶת חֲבֵרוֹ
בַּדֶּרֶךְ הַיָּשָׁר וְהָרָצוּי לְפָנֶיךָ, וְאַל יַעֲלֶה שׁוּם שִׂנְאָה
מֵאֶחָד עַל חֲבֵרוֹ, חָלִילָה. וּתְחַזֵּק הִתְקַשְּׁרוּתֵנוּ
בְּאַהֲבָה אֵלֶיךָ. כַּאֲשֶׁר גָּלוּי וְיָדוּעַ לְפָנֶיךָ, שֶׁיְּהֵא
הַכֹּל נַחַת-רוּחַ אֵלֶיךָ...אָמֵן, כֵּן יְהִי רָצוֹן.

On the contrary, place it in our hearts that we see the good things in our companions and not their weaknesses, and that we speak with everyone in a way that is straightforward and acceptable before You. Do not raise in our hearts any feelings of hatred toward people, God forbid, but strengthen our connection to You with love, just as it has been revealed before You, that all should be joyous before You... Amen, so it should be Your will.

Recommended Reading

The Quill of the Heart, published by the Chofetz Chaim Heritage Foundation

Tales of the Tongue, by Esther Ehrenreich and Chaya Kahan

The Gift of Speech, by Rav Shimon Finkelman

We Want Life, by Yisrael Greenwald, illustrated by Getzel

A Twist of the Tongue, by Menachem Moshe Oppen

Guard Your Tongue, by Rabbi Zelig Pliskin

The Power of Words, by Rabbi Zelig Pliskin

It Wasn't How It Seemed, by Rebbetzin Yehudis Samet

The Other Side of the Story, by Rebbetzin Yehudis Samet

Courtrooms of the Mind, by Rabbi Hanoch Teller

Glossary

Aggadah — Homiletic passages.

Am Yisrael — The nation of Israel.

Anan hakavod — Cloud of glory.

Avinu — Our father.

Avodah zarah — Idol worship.

Be'ezras Hashem — God willing (with God's help).

B'nei Yisrael — The children of Israel.

Chalilah — Heaven forbid.

Chilul Hashem — The desecration of God's Name.

Chazal — Acronym for "*Chachameinu zichronam liverachah*" — Our Sages of blessed memory.

Chesed — Acts of lovingkindness.

Chupah — Wedding canopy.

Chumash — Five books of the Torah.

Divrei kodesh — Hallowed speech.

Eretz Yisrael — The land of Israel.

Gematria — The numbers attributed to the letters of the *alef-beis* which give additional insights into the scriptures.

Gezel — A form of theft.

Haggadah — The story of Passover read at the seder.

Halachah — Jewish law.

Hashem — God.

Hashem Yisbarach — God, may He be blessed.

Hashgachah pratis — Divine providence.

Haskamah — Approbation.

Kabbalah — Jewish mysticism.

Kefirah — Heresy.

Kesubah — Jewish marriage contract.

Klal Yisrael — All the Jewish people.

Imeinu — Our mother.

Ivri — Hebrew (n).

Kal vachomer — Then even more so.

Lashon hakodesh — The holy language, Hebrew.

Lashon hara — Evil speech.

Machzor — Type of prayerbook.

Middah keneged middah — In the same way; measure for measure.

Midrash — Traditional teaching.

Minchah — Afternoon prayer.

Mishkan — Tabernacle.

Mitzvah — Commandment (also good deed).

Motzi shem ra — Making up a story that isn't true and makes the subject look bad.

Nissayon — Test or trial, usually of a spiritual nature.

Ona'as devarim — Words which cause the hearer pain.

Parashah — Weekly Torah portion.

Pasuk — Verse.

Perush — Interpretation.

Pesach — Passover.

Pikuach nefesh — A matter of life and death.

Rabbeinu — Our teacher.

Rishonim — The early commentators of the Talmud.

Ruach hakodesh — Divine Inspiration.

Rechilus — Gossip.

Sanhedrin — The early court of the Jewish people in Talmudic times.

Shalom bayis — Marital harmony.

Shecht — Ritually slaughter.

Shemiras halashon — Guarding one's speech.

Shemittah — The Sabbatical year.

Shidduch — Marriage prospect.

Shiur — Lesson.

Siyata diShmaya — Divine assistance.

Tikkun — Fixing, usually of oneself to right past misdeeds.

Yetzer hara — The evil inclination.

Zechus — Merit.